Sweethearts

of

'60s TV

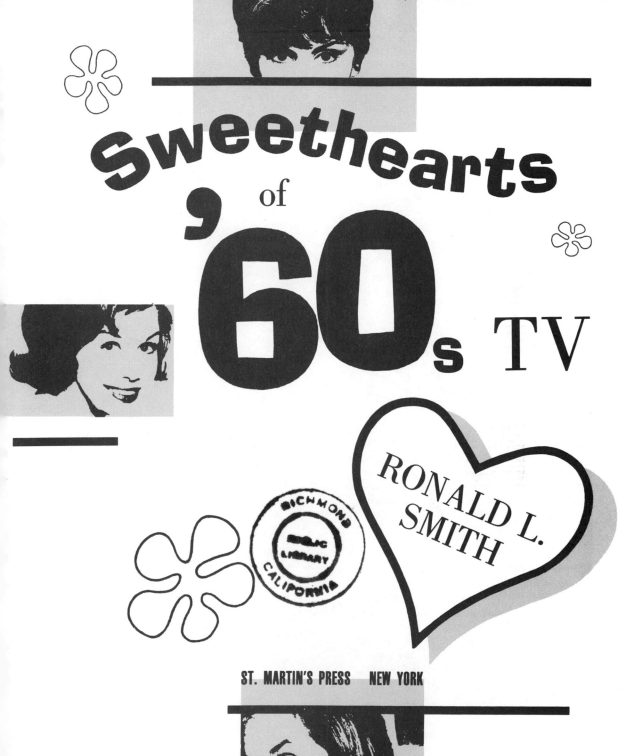

Sweethearts of '60s TV

RONALD L. SMITH

ST. MARTIN'S PRESS   NEW YORK

Design by Judith Stagnitto

Library of Congress Cataloging-in-Publication Data

Smith, Ronald L., 1952–
   Sweethearts of '60s TV.
   1. Women in television—United States—History.
2. Television actors and actresses—United States—
Biography. I. Title. II. Title: Sweethearts of sixties TV.
PN1992.8.W65S58 1989   791.45′028′0922
88–30552
ISBN 0–312–02649–8 (pbk.)

First Edition
10 9 8 7 6 5 4 3 2 1

Contents

Introduction

Who were "The Sweethearts of '60s TV"?

They were the women who were the role models for a generation.

Aside from family members and teachers, these women were the ones we learned from.

We grew up watching them every week—sometimes every day in reruns—looking for entertainment and discovering "ideal women." Women girls wanted to emulate. Girls guys wanted to marry.

They were . . .

THE GIRLS NEXT DOOR

We learned about dating from Marlo Thomas as Ann Marie. Dawn Wells was the ideal role model for the all-American girl. We learned kindness from Donna Douglas as Elly May. Teenage lifestyles were mirrored by Sally Field as Gidget.

DREAM WIVES

We grew up believing the ideal housewife was Mary Tyler Moore as Laura Petrie. Adding a dash of fantasy was Elizabeth Montgomery—"bewitched" but still another image of what a dream housewife was like. And there was Eva Gabor, who showed that a love partnership was worth any sacrifice, even living in Green Acres.

COMIC CUTIES

They made us laugh—but there was more. Judy Carne and Goldie Hawn's elfin and innocent sexiness gave us our first hints of the erotic revolution in the '60s. Meanwhile on *Get Smart*, many found in Barbara Feldon a winning combination of allure, good nature, and good humor.

 ## FANTASY FIGURES

Our image of the sensual woman was fired up by red-headed Tina Louise and the bottled-up blond genie, Barbara Eden. Those looking for perfection found their ultimate dream girl in the very real Julie Newmar—both brain and body.

 ## WOMEN OF ACTION

The '60s saw women become a force in occupations formerly for men only, even the dangerous profession of spy. Stefanie Powers began it with *The Girl from U.N.C.L.E.*, along with Anne Francis as Honey West and, ultimately, Diana Rigg as Emma Peel.

They were all special. The '60s was a special time. There were interesting TV stars in the '50s, '70s, and '80s, but never so many as in the '60s.

What generation can boast a "sweet sixteen" of such fondly remembered stars? How many shows endure as well as those from the '60s?

What made these women so successful? What were the qualities they had

that enthralled and inspired young men and women? Why are their shows still so popular in rerun? How did these fantasy girls of the '60s survive to become women of the '80s?

It would take a book twice this size to cover all the intriguing questions about these remarkable women. But in the space allowed, here's some nostalgia about their shows, a profile of their lives, and a look at the fantasy of what they represented then and the reality of who they are now.

For space reasons, the author chose a "sweet sixteen." To try and include more would've made the profiles "thumbnail," or even lower—footnotes.

The thinning-out process began with the decade itself. Some stars, like Tuesday Weld, Connie Stevens, and Dorothy Provine, were closer to the '50s. Others, like Peggy Lipton and Barbara Bain, were closer to the '70s.

Then there was the question of influence. Some women appeared in the '60s (Jill Ireland on *Shane*, Linda Evans on *Big Valley*, Mariette Hartley on *The Hero*, Patty Duke on *The Patty Duke Show*, Mia Farrow on *Peyton Place*, and Barbara Hershey on *The Monroes*) but made more of an impression elsewhere in their careers.

Some women just didn't get much of a chance to show their stuff, though they did have many loyal fans: Melody Patterson (*F Troop*); Julie Parrish (*Good Morning World*); Veronica Cartwright (*Daniel Boone*); all the various daughters on *Petticoat Junction*; Pat Priest, the nice-looking blonde on *The Munsters* during most of its run; Marta Kristen, the blonde on *Lost in Space*; Michelle Nichols, the nice-looking black on *Star Trek*; and Carol Merrill, who pioneered the art of quiz-show womanhood on *Let's Make a Deal*. And there were quite a few fans who had a ghoulish fascination with Carolyn Jones on *The Addams Family* and Yvonne De-Carlo on *The Munsters!*

The author, an impressionable fan in the '60s, wrote to many of these women, treasuring the photos and letters received, fascinated by all the various qualities they represented in "ideal womanhood." Like many others, he consciously or subconsciously found qualities in them that he would look for in a girlfriend.

Part of the inspiration for the book came from looking through some memorabilia on one of these '60s stars, and realizing that there were quite a few similarities between that "dream girl" of the '60s and his own ultimate choice of a "woman of the '80s."

It is sad that there are so few role models now for the impressionable kids to respond to the way the '60s generation did to their TV sweethearts. How many of today's stars have the morality these stars did, the responsibility to their fans, the dedication to their roles even if they were merely starring in "a harmless sitcom"?

Happily, the story of most of these TV sweethearts is not a sad one. As women of the '80s, the majority have fulfilled the promise of that golden decade. The '60s promised creative freedom. These women have taken command of that freedom to fulfill ambitions of producing films, writing books, owning businesses, and reaching out to others. Some have enjoyed the freedom of being able to remain the same—to thumb their noses (and beautiful faces) at "middle age" and remain forever young.

The '60s was an exciting time—also a painful, even frightening time. These stars made it a good time to grow up.

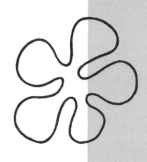

Girls Next Door

Dawn Wells

GILLIGAN'S ISLAND

First broadcast: September 26, 1964
Last broadcast: September 4, 1967

In a way, Mary Ann of *Gilligan's Island* was the truest "sweetheart" of '60s TV. While most sweethearts were supernatural, super-spies, or slight exaggerations of country girls (Elly May), city girls (Ann Marie), or beach girls (Gidget), Mary Ann Summers was pure '60s Americana, a simple, unspoiled girl from Horners Corners, Kansas.

The part of Mary Ann was played by Dawn Wells—pure Americana herself. Dawn's great-great grandfather drove a stage coach from Reno to Virginia City during the Gold Rush. She was born in Reno, Nevada (October 18). Her father didn't own Wells Fargo, but he did own a trucking company called Wells Cargo.

Dawn planned to become a ballerina, but trick knees ended that dream. Her knees looked good, at least, and the rest of her looked great. She became Miss Nevada, and participated in the 1960 Miss America contest. "I thought it would be a good experience to get in front of an audience and maintain that kind of composure," she says now. "I never had any idea that I'd win. It was a wonderful experience doing the Miss America pageant."

Like the other Miss Americas of that era, Dawn was a true model for America's youth. She was not only beautiful, but bright—treasurer of the student body in school and a member of the debate team.

"I was very puritanical," she recalls. "I didn't really drink, and of course there were no drug problems then. I was very square. I was very much Mary Ann, I think that the soul of Mary Ann was very much in essence me. I was raised very strictly. My parents were divorced—I was very close to both of them but I lived with my mother who was very strict with me. I couldn't get away with anything, not that I would've." Like her character Mary Ann, Dawn was a sweet, sensible girl. Mary Ann and the Professor were the most logical and capable inhabitants of Gilligan's Island.

A chemistry major at Stephens College in Missouri, Dawn later switched to drama. After getting her AA at the two-year college, she went on to a BA in drama at the University of Washington. "One of the hardest things starting the acting was eliminating the chemistry side of me and just concentrating on the emotional, artistic side of me, 'cause I'm a very practical person, and I tend to think things through. When you act you should 'be it,' not 'think it.' So in preparing how my life was going to go I said I'd try to be an actress and I'd give myself a year."

Though she had very few credits—(a star of summer stock at the Pink Garter Theater in Jackson Hole, Wyoming), she found work easily. "I hate to admit that because it brings false hopes to the poor kids thinking of going into the business, but I came here and got an agent within six weeks and got my first job within six weeks."

She was in a play called *Black-Eyed Susan* with Mercedes McCambridge and Leon Ames. Later she appeared in the film *The New Interns* and became friends with costar Barbara Eden. On TV shows like *Burke's Law* and *Wagon Train*, she was usually cast as "the ingenue. I played a couple of hookers, but not many."

When *Gilligan's Island* came along, Dawn didn't grab it. She didn't know about it. They filmed the pilot without her! The original half hour concerned Gilligan, the skipper, and their two rich passengers. The other characters were minor. As Dawn recalls it, "In the original, Mary Ann, Ginger, and the Professor were three schoolteachers I think. CBS or [producer] Sherwood Schwartz, I'm not sure which, decided to give it a little more variety, and make the characters different. Tina, Russell, and myself didn't do the pilot. I know that John Gabriel was the Professor, and that one of the girls was played by Kit Smythe, but I don't remember what the other girl's name was." Dawn came aboard as luckless Mary Ann—marooned on her first trip away from home.

When the reviews came in, everybody on the island was luckless. Sherwood Schwartz had chosen the name Gilligan out of a phone book, hunting for a funny name that would immediately indicate the show was a comedy. The critics still didn't know.

"It is impossible that a more inept, moronic or humorless show has ever appeared on the home tube," wrote UPI critic Rick DuBrow. The show was ridiculed as the ultimate example of how TV quality had degenerated.

At the time, Bob Denver had to admit that *Gilligan's Island* was not exactly bril-

♥ Cheerful islander: the standard bikini publicity pose . . . and the autographed picture sent to the author and other '60s fans.

liant TV: "It doesn't take a mature intellect to laugh at a monkey running off with Gilligan's dinner or a guy getting hit on the head by a coconut."

With most of the slapstick centered on Gilligan and the Skipper, with dizzy bickering from Mr. Howell and his wife, and movie star Ginger Grant providing the breathtaking scenery, it seemed that the last two characters, Mary Ann and the Professor, had little to do. In fact, they were merely "the rest" as far as the show's theme song was concerned. But soon the producers realized that Mary Ann was an important cast member, too.

"I always thought in my mind, here's Ginger, this beautiful girl, this sexy girl, and of course that's where the male attention is going to go," says Dawn today. "I didn't know until this year [1988] that I got the most fan mail. I assumed Gilligan would've, or the young men writing to Tina. I got the most fan mail, which surprised me, but I realize now that I was everybody's kind of girl next door, a fantasy but not fantasy—the reality is that you could probably approach Mary Ann, and she might be the girl you take home to mother, or that you might tell your troubles to."

Ginger Grant could make men swoon—a perfumed beauty in slinky gowns. But Mary Ann was a breath of

5

fresh air in sporty short shorts. In fact, the show's censors were worried more about Dawn than Tina! "Just like Barbara Eden on *Jeannie*, I couldn't show my navel. The shorts had to be high cut." The alternative was to wear her other trademark costume, the gingham skirt.

Dawn recalls getting a plentiful amount of puppy-love mail from boys who wanted to marry her, and thousands of letters from girls asking for beauty tips on how to have such wonderful curly hair. She laughs lightly: "I also got an awful lot of sexy dirty fan mail! I still do. I get letters with religious overtones—about what a good girl Mary Ann is. And then they start talking about your legs, and your chest! These letters combine goodness and sexuality. I didn't think Mary Ann was the sex image, I thought Ginger was, but I did get a great amount of these letters, and I've had some kind of dangerous experiences. I think it's because people feel they can approach me. And if they feel they can approach you they assume you're going to accept them, and you have to be very careful how you reject them."

While some may have fantasized about matching themselves with Dawn Wells, the big preoccupation with *Gilligan's Island* fans in general was trying to figure out likely matches among the lost islanders. Who might've been sleeping with whom?

Would Mary Ann have gone for Gilligan? The Skipper? Logic would favor the Professor . . .

"That's interesting," says Dawn. "There was some matchmaking with Gilligan and Mary Ann also. The Howells tried to match us up and get us engaged at one point, but I think everything became taboo because of censorship. Here were all these people on the island and nobody's watching where the girls are sleeping and the boys are sleeping. The Howells were married, which helped some, but that whole sexual innuendo was just left untouched." She laughs. "This was pre–Norman Lear! I'd love to see what *Gilligan's Island* would be now, we'd all be living in the same hut. I don't know!

"Now what Mary Ann would do? I don't know. I think she'd be very understanding and forgiving of Gilligan, and protective of him, and yet I think there would be a tremendous amount of respect for the Professor, so I don't know what she'd do . . ."

In real life, Dawn married agent Larry Rosen, but it lasted just about as long as the show.

For three years, sweet Mary Ann and the rest of the islanders enjoyed good ratings. The show left the air due to a scheduling conflict. CBS had dropped *Gunsmoke* and replaced it with *Mannix*. When viewers protested, CBS had to bring it back. The half hour after *Gilligan's Island* was still unscheduled, so it was an easy decision to ax *Gilligan*, add the free half hour, and bring back Marshal Dillon. How many viewers and newspaper critics would dare defend their slapstick sitcom? Today a network thinks twice about canceling a show in the Top 20 or Top 30, but back then networks often dropped shows on the basis of demographics *(Red Skelton)*, politics *(The Smothers Brothers)*, or image *(Gilligan's Island)*.

It was a rough few months. Scripts had been bought and the cast had fully expected to start filming. The news of the cancellation came in March. In May, Dawn's father died. She appeared in a few TV episodes, including an installment of *The Invaders*, but her practical side emerged again, and she decided not to pursue TV.

"I thought basically after *Gilligan's Island* I'd be playing the character of Mary Ann for the next ten years if I didn't stretch some more. You get typed pretty easily. So I did national tours, regional theater, and dinner theater." She made two films in 1977, *Return to Boggy Creek* and *The Town That Dreaded Sundown*. On stage, she veered from comedy to play Ava Gardner's part in *Night of the Iguana*. Her favorite role was in *The Effect of Gamma Rays on Man-in-the-Moon Marigolds*. She took the challenge of musicals *(They're Playing Our Song)*, won fine reviews in *Bell, Book and Candle*, *The Owl and the Pussycat*, and *Chapter Two*, and is also proud of doing a thriller called *Fatal Attraction* in 1986 (no relation to the 1987 movie).

She's been very busy guesting on TV shows lately, including *Alf*, *Growing Pains*, and *Matlock*.

She always had to be wary of critics who knew her only as Mary Ann. "Always. Always. They usually come with an attitude because of it: 'Prove it to me.' Because most of the critics are still making fun of *Gilligan's Island*."

Most critics who see her praise her—while still panning the past: "Never mind that Dawn Wells played Mary Ann in 'Gilligan's Island,' the *Minneapolis Tribune* wrote of her role in *Chapter Two*, "she's a brilliant actress with a superb sense of timing."

"When I do a role it's real important to me that what I'm doing has quality. Because everyone will come see Mary Ann one time—what does she look like now, what's she like in person—but unless they come away having enjoyed the play and feeling all the communication that happens in the theater, they're not going to come back and see you. I've been lucky—'cause I really—knock on wood—have not been out of work except by choice since the series went off the air, and that's pretty tough to say in this day and age."

During nearly fifteen years of theatrical touring, Dawn called Nashville her home base. She had a steady relationship for all those years with Tom Ervin. It was a slightly unorthodox partnership. "We never lived together or anything. We both had our own lives kind of. It was sort of a nice arrangement, we're no longer together but it was nice. He was a lovely man, and I'm very close to his children. Since I don't have children that was an important part for me. It was certainly unconventional I suppose, but we both had our own lives and we were committed to each other as if we were married, there was never any of that playing around kind of stuff."

Then why didn't she marry? "Truthfully both of us were very into what we were doing and I feel to be a wife you should be there all the time and I was out of town for three weeks or three months, and I don't think you can take on the responsibilities of a wife and do that. So our arrangement was adequate for both of us."

She came back to California in March 1987, tired of the constant touring, eager for something new. Oddly, in one of the last *Gilligan* TV movies, Mary Ann also had the chance for marriage, and balked. "She went back home on one of our specials to marry her old-time sweetheart— she was committed to go through it and didn't—that's kind of Mary Ann. She would be the one helping milk the cows,

♥ **Dawn today—glamorous star and successful businesswoman.**

helping make decisions on the farm. She wouldn't sit back and be taken care of. She wouldn't be Lovey [Mrs. Howell on the show]. She would be a contributor. I don't think that like Dawn Wells she's overly aggressive or overly unfeminine. I'm not a women's libber in the case that I have to prove that I'm better than a man. I think women can do a lot of things equally as well as a man, but I sure still like being a woman, I think there are advantages to both sexes, that they ought to keep them in their place. I mean I'm a believer in just everybody being self-reliant. You have to answer to yourself first, and then when your cup is full, and when you're a full person, the love can be given to someone else. I don't believe you should take something away from someone else to make you a complete person. Two happy people make a happy couple, not one unhappy person trying to get the happiness from the other. That's unhealthy I think. I hope someday to remarry. I'm not antimarriage at all. I believe in love and I believe in a relationship and a commitment and all of that, very much so. But I also like making my own decisions."

In her career, Dawn's decision seems to be diversity. She's enjoying her work as an actress. She's also been active in teaching advanced acting courses at Stephens College in Missouri, her old alma mater. She also is a clothing designer. Her fashions are practical, attractive—and for very special people. "The fellow that I was going with in Nashville, his mother was in a nursing home for ten years. The ladies have their bathrobes turned around backward so they can get them on—and there's no dignity or self-respect. They don't feel good about themselves. Finally I asked myself why? Why do we treat our senior citizens like that? So I designed these cheerful, pretty bathrobes and nightshirts. They open down the back and are easily accessible, washable and durable. I think it's something that's really needed." She got the idea when she was appearing in *They're Playing Our Song,* and her costume—a skirt, blouse, and sweater—were all one piece, attached in the back with Velcro for quick changes between scenes. "And I thought, Why can't you make this costume work for these people? So that's kind of what

I've done. I'm very excited about it."

At one time, a woman in her late forties or early fifties seemed old. There's nothing old about Dawn, who has a vivacious personality, a charming and frequent laugh, and hardly looks her age. She believes in fitness. "I like water aerobics a lot, the pressure of the water kind of contours your body, I think. I also think swimming is one of the best things for your body. I also have a rowing machine I use. I'm not a health nut, but all my life I've been a real balanced food eater, I've dieted all my life. My father was very big and very tall, my mother's very little. I always felt I'd be my mother's height and my father's weight, so from day one I was always very nutrition-conscious of what's good for you and what isn't. I also think it's partly hereditary. I'm part Italian, and I think the Italian side of me, with the oils in the skin and all of that, helps too. Contrary to what everybody says, I'm a sun worshipper—I know that's terrible, but I like a little color. I believe in water, I drink a lot of water.

"I consider myself to be very fortunate that I've been working so much and so long. A pianist doesn't play the piano once a year and think he's wonderful—you've got to keep at it, you've got to keep growing, and you've got to keep improving, but that's the beauty and the joy of art to me, that's the creative process. I can't sit idle. There are a lot of aspects to me that need fulfilling. Maybe part of it's because I have not had children and a family, so that there's another area that needs to be taken up, the slack needs to be taken up a little, but I'm a very happy person. I'm very fortunate, and I'm real content with my life. I like where I am and who I am, and that's a good sign."

Recently she took a trip to Africa, joining climbers on an excursion to the lair of mountain gorillas. "I climbed from eight thousand to twelve thousand feet in one day, hacking through the jungle, and I got ten feet from the silverback gorilla and the whole family. Even now I get goose bumps—it's like taking yourself back to prehistoric times. This five-hundred-pound creature looking you in the eye—no hostility—gentleness, curiosity, total trust. It was really something, it almost changes your life. I've traveled a lot, to Russia and all of that, but Africa—that was a real experience for me."

It seems that no matter how often Dawn has been around the world, she inevitably ends up back on Gilligan's Island. There have been three TV movies so far, and constant talk of another. She doesn't mind. In fact, it's these movies that help keep the cast so close. For over twenty years now, the various Gilligan's Islanders have remained friends. "Oh absolutely," Dawn says. "Alan Hale and I had lunch together yesterday as a matter of fact. Natalie Schafer and I are quite good friends. I adore Bob [Denver] and his wife. They don't live in town though. He's really kind of shy, something of a loner. And I see Russell, of course. Jim [Backus] has not been very well so I haven't seen him very much, or Tina, since she's done none of our specials."

Though the various members of the show have been quoted as bitter about the lack of residuals (the standard contract at the time called for payment for only the first five reruns of each episode), Dawn, true to her Mary Ann spirit, looks on the bright side. "The residuals we got probably doubled the salary we made. Yeah, somebody else is making a lot more money off it now, but because it's on the air you're able to make money somewhere else.

"We didn't plan a strategy," she admits. "We didn't think about merchandising dolls and posters. We were doing a show, that's what we were doing. Nowadays you might do it a little differently—you know you've got to capture the time you're on the air and make the most of it, but I think I've made a living because of *Gilligan*'s popularity. My price has gone up, my choices are different. I'm not saying that it isn't a hindrance in some ways too. It's a double-edged sword I suppose.

"I have good memories, good feelings, it was a wonderful experience. It wasn't the most creative acting job I ever had, but I loved the character, I loved the experience of doing it, and I went on. I don't have any hostile feelings about it. I have such an animosity for actors who get on a series and then bad-rap it. 'It's a piece of garbage, I wish I were out doing Shakespeare.' Then why take the job away from some actor that would love to do it? Why try to sabotage something that others are working hard at? If you don't want to work on television then don't do it!"

Dawn still gets about fifty fan letters a week from *Gilligan* fans old and new. "It's kind of nice. Some fans follow you through it all, send me Christmas cards, and when I'm on the road they come and see me. I was doing a show and afterward a whole family came to see me backstage. One of them said, 'I watched you when I was growing up, my parents loved you, my children are now watching you.' So you have three generations watching you. That's something. We've never been off the air in twenty-three years," she adds with a laugh, "if you could stand it!"

She seems to be able to stand the constant *Gilligan* reminders. "I got on the plane last year in Disney World, coming out of Orlando flying into Atlanta, and the entire Eastern Airlines plane broke into the *Gilligan's Island* song! [Laughs] I mean . . . it was twenty-three years ago! My fantasy is going to a costume party as Mary Ann in my gingham dress, gray pigtails, and a walker. How long can we do this!"

She admits that every now and then she'll catch a rerun. "It's really kind of fun how it holds up—nonsensical silly slapstick humor is what it was. Escapism is all it was, but it was one of the best there was." It was the ultimate escapist show—people trying to escape the island every week. But with Mary Ann on the island, there was also good reason to stay.

Donna Douglas

THE BEVERLY HILLBILLIES

First broadcast: September 26, 1962
Last broadcast: September 7, 1971

"Is Elly May ready?" a suitor asks Granny Clampett.

"She shor is! She's been ready since she was fourteen!"

Elly May Clampett: luscious with a peaches-and-cream complexion and strawberry blond hair. She had an innocence that belied what was blossoming under that checked shirt and rope-tied pair of blue jeans. Not exactly a simple farmer's daughter, Elly May Clampett had some titillating contradictions. She had some traits that made her seem easy: she was a well-built, naïve blonde eager for a beau. But she was not so easy— she had old-fashioned country morals, she startled guys by becoming the gleeful aggressor, and she was usually equal to them in strength.

Though Elly May Clampett may have been inspired by Daisy Mae, the "Li'l Abner" delight, Donna Douglas made the role more than one-dimensional. Elly May was not only a gosh-durn beauty, she was *real*. Donna's sweetness, innocence, and charm were no act. When producer Paul Henning asked her if she could play the part, she smiled and said, "Could I handle Elly May? Why, it's just like my own life."

Donna Douglas was born Doris Smith, near Pride, Louisiana. The generally accepted birthdate is September 26, 1939—exactly twenty-three years before *The Beverly Hillbillies* premiered on CBS.

Pride, Louisiana, was a small community, "a store and maybe two or three houses." Donna was a down-home girl who knew how to milk a cow, slop hogs, and whistle through her teeth. She was very much the tomboy. Eventually she and the family (she had a plentiful brood of brothers, but no sisters) moved on to the nearest big city: Baywood, Louisiana. As a girl, Donna ate the same cuisine that Granny would later shock America with: possum innards, collard greens, and hog jowls.

On the show, Granny once said, "When a girl passes fourteen she's an old maid. When she passes sixteen she's a spinster. When she's over eighteen—forget it!"

Back in Louisiana, Donna wasn't about to forget it. At seventeen, she got herself hitched to one Roland Bourgeois. She had a son by him named Danny. As she recalls, "We were too young. We spent most of the time playing baseball." The marriage ended quickly.

Donna was by far the prettiest girl in Baywood High School, and was soon winning beauty prizes. The bayou girl got herself gussied up to win the title of Miss New Orleans in 1957, and Miss Baton Rouge the following year. She tried out for most any contest that came her way, even if it was just Miss Hot Pepper. When she entered that one, and discovered part of the competition included eating hot peppers, she just went ahead and chowed down. She won that one fair and square, appeared on local TV, and even did some commercials for the folks who made the peppers.

She went to New York, where she found work as a model, mostly for artists and illustrators. She augmented this with some minor TV exposure. She was a "billboard girl" for *The Steve Allen Show*, and a "letters girl" for Perry Como. She didn't have much to do except look pretty, but she did that extremely well. In fact, the country girl was even winning beauty contests against sophisticated city women. When a group of newspapermen chose her as Miss Byline, she somehow ended up on *The Ed Sullivan Show*.

Producer Hal Wallis happened to be watching, and signed up the young Louisiana belle for a movie called *Career*, starring Shirley MacLaine. It wasn't a career, but it was a start. Once in Hollywood, Donna appeared in more movies, from a bit in *Li'l Abner* to the part of Tony Randall's secretary in *Lover Come Back*. She appeared on TV in everything from *The Jack Benny Show* to *The Untouchables*.

From the start, coworkers could see that this unspoiled girl from the South was "the real thing." She wasn't the typical starlet. She was quiet, introspective, and philosophical. When it came time to cast *The Beverly Hillbillies*, Paul Henning remembered Donna from the Tony Randall movie. The clincher that vaulted her over the 150 other Ellys was her strength. The busty hillbilly gal really was robust, and despite a bout of whiplash from a recent car accident, when they asked her if she could lift up an actor for a comic scene, she plumb carried him across her back!

When *The Beverly Hillbillies* premiered on her birthday in 1962, it was roasted by

number 1 in the country, and the Clampett clan were pictured as some kind of Joad family—riding to California over TV's barren, dusty, "vast wasteland."

Producer Paul Henning, defending the show almost every day, insisted that the Clampetts were "warm human beings. Funny, but with a certain dignity. Viewers like 'em, and that's that."

Despite all the pressure and strain of "instant stardom," Donna managed to remain unspoiled. "It's impossible to get into an argument with her," Henning told reporters. "She's all tranquility and peace. Donna has found a religion which gives her unbelievable serenity. I've never seen anyone so adjusted."

Buddy Ebsen recalls now, "Like her character, Donna was a tomboy who blossomed into a beautiful young woman." He smiles wryly. "In fact she had to relearn the accent she once fought to get rid of."

Donna's warmth and goodness were reflected in Elly May. She was a sweetheart who showed tenderness toward animals, and respect for her elders. She didn't exaggerate her sex appeal as the "Li'l Abner" women had. In fact, all she had to do was stand there. Gilbert Seldes, in a 1962 *TV Guide*, insisted, "It is a pleasure to follow the camera dotingly along her figure from head to bare feet." Indeed, decades before suggestive jeans ads, Donna's tight pants were unique.

most of the critics. The *Saturday Evening Post* believed the show "aimed low and hit its target." Many saw the series as proof that quality TV was heading down the drain in the '60s, after the brief nobility of late-'50s live teledramas. *Time* magazine was outraged by the corny country comedy, insisting "the pone is the lowest form of humor." *The New York Times* said the show was "too absurd to be even slightly amusing," and picked *I'm Dickens, He's Fenster* to be "the surprise success" of the new season.

The big surprise was that within five weeks, the new hillbilly comedy was

As Elly, Donna displayed charm and frisky good nature. She gave almost every line a peppy, spunky delivery. Of course, her sheer physical presence was enough. Jack O'Brien, writing in the New York *Journal American*, on April 17, 1963, believed Donna "to be TV's answer to Brigitte Bardot, or possibly the sexy hillbilly cartoons in the barber shop magazines . . . her popularity is based on . . . the chance that any or all of her buttons might pop."

For 1962, Elly was very much a typical young girl who wanted to go on dates but didn't seem to want to go all the way. Naïve huggin' and kissin' was just fine. Young girls could relate to Elly, even if instead of stuffed animals she had real ones. For boys, she was a dream girl, especially since the dreams were fairly innocent. Just to go down to the see-ment pond and maybe skinny dip was about as dirty a thought as one could have about Elly.

For 1962, Elly was an interesting, half-liberated figure. She was stronger than most men; when one tried to kiss her hand, she flipped him over, insisting, "He was fixin' to bite me." She was cheerfully aggressive, whether pursuing any nice young feller who happened along, or a full-fledged movie star like Dash Riprock. Girls could find something far beyond ladylike Barbie-doll mannerisms in Elly May. Though she looked good in gingham dresses, she more often wore jeans, which was pretty daring for an age where jeans were definitely not okay to wear at school. And Elly would've burned her bra—but instead used it as a "dou-ble-barreled sling shot." It's no wonder that, of all the Hillbillies, Donna got the most mail.

Paul Henning remembers, "She asked me rather timidly if she could have a little help in answering some, and I found she had about six thousand stashed in a box." After a day at the studio, Donna would go to her small apartment ten blocks away and study her script for the next day. "She never blows a line," Buddy Ebsen said. "The hardest-working young actress I've ever seen." Then she would personally answer her fan mail. Eventually she would send out stamped color postcards, but only because the demand became too much for her to handle. She lived alone, except for Frances, her parakeet. It was named after St. Francis of Assisi.

Elly May Clampett's love of animals seemed so genuine because Donna Douglas had a definite rapport with them. A vegetarian, she said, "I respect animals—I feel their vibrations." When an episode called for Elly to hug a bear, Paul Henning was ready with a stand-in, but Donna insisted on doing the scene herself.

While fame could apply a lethal bear hug itself, Donna seemed to be able to handle the show's monumental success—the number 1 series in 1963 and 1964, and a Top 20 show for the next six years. Her placidity was reflected in sayings. She always had one for a specific question. "You can have success if you can

♥ **Elly gets Granny's goat.**

handle it," she believed. When asked about achieving inner peace, she explained that studying the Bible was a good place to start, claiming it was the best place to learn a big lesson: "Know thyself."

Donna studied metaphysics. She told writer Liza Wilson, "Metaphysics is the awareness of the mind beyond the pure physical relationship. I believe that all things have a meaning in life and that whatever you do creates the total you. Everything is part of an individual. I am striving to be a total person." About the only thing Donna was hesitant about, at that stage, was her age. "Age is a state of mind," she'd say. "I'm asked to play an eighteen-year-old girl on the show and that's what I am."

Donna received tremendous publicity right from the start. *TV Guide* did a pictorial on her, proclaiming "Donna Douglas did more for blue jeans in seven months than cowboys did in 110 years." In fact, one episode was about how Elly was turned down by a snobby girls' school—until she turned their heads around and blue jeans became the latest fashion. In another episode, she was given a fancy ball gown, and she did the most natural thing in the world—she went out and played ball in it.

On *The Beverly Hillbillies Original Cast Album* from Columbia, fans could listen to Elly vocalizing on a few duets. Granny tries to teach her about "The Birds and the Bees." Elly: "I know the birds and the bees, I learned that when I was young. The bees

is the little ones." Granny: "That's all ya know! Elly, you're gonna get stung!"

Over the years, the show not only retained its success, but won converts. *TV Guide* in 1966 noted that Donna still "filled her blue jeans to perfection . . . what makes the show both durable and endurable is an utter lack of pretension."

Folks tuned in every week, watching the "comic strip humor" of the show—where Granny would tell Jethro to "dress the turkey" and he'd come back with a turkey in a suit. Where the ringing of a doorbell seemed like a sign of ghosts. Where the family ate in "the fancy eatin' room" on a billiard table. And where an old "Li'l Abner" expression kept cropping up: "Don't that take the rag off'n the bush!"

♥ **Another critter for animal crack-ups fun.**

Donna occasionally got a chance to show off her figure in a party dress (Pa: "She's slicker 'n a cow's belly!"). There would inevitably be a long shot of her sauntering down the staircase like a debutante, accompanied by elegant, but roller-rink-style organ music. In fact, for one "classic" episode that united all of Paul Henning's hit shows, she and the Clampetts journeyed to Hooterville where, gussied up in a light blue sheath of a gown, complete with white stole, she dazzled the three Bradley girls of *Petticoat Junction* and even outshone Lisa Douglas of *Green Acres*.

In one classic episode, an oily Arab sheikh gives Jed four harem girls (all in full costumes, doing writhing belly dances). But they don't have a fourth of the appeal of tousle-haired Elly. When the sheikh sees her, he's staggered: "Her face is so fair as to confuse the sun, her hair a cascade of golden moonlight. Her eyes, twin pools of rapture!"

Elly is surprised. "Who's he talkin' about, Jethro?"

Jethro: "Dogged if I know!"

The sheikh is ready to swap two hundred sheep, two hundred goats, fifty horses, one thousand pieces of gold, and a camel for her. ("Sorriest lookin' horse I ever did see," Jed says of the camel.) Of course, the offer is not nearly as tempting as Elly May. When the sheikh attempts to make off with her anyway, she beats him black and blue. "American wildcat!" he cries.

The only "competition" Donna ever really had on *The Beverly Hillbillies* was during the first year of the show, when there were occasional glimpses of one of banker Drysdale's attractive secretaries—Janet Trego—played by Sharon Tate.

As the star of TV's favorite show, and one of the most energetic symbols of womanhood on the tube, Donna could have her pick of admirers. She remained demure. "I'm not thinking of getting married again," she said in 1965, "but if I found somebody I was interested in, I'd adjust. But I don't socialize a lot. I don't go out a lot. I still get a little shy."

Fans surprised her. Though she and the other Hillbillies made many personal appearance tours, and raked in big bucks doing the county fair circuit in the summer, she was often shocked by the enthusiasm and love the fans showed. Once, coming out of a church on a visit back to Louisiana, she found a throng of people waiting to get a glimpse of her, folks who had driven all the way from Mississippi having heard she was in the area.

The formula for the sitcom varied slightly through the '60s. Sometimes the Clampetts brought their hillbilly ways to a fresh location, like England. But mostly the show's 215 episodes were pretty uniform. Trying to make it into the '70s, one sitcom plot involved women's lib—with Granny refusing to make coffee for Jed, and Elly running around with a sign for GRUN: "Girls Resist Unfair Neglect."

It wasn't working. When the show faded out at the start of the '70s, it was for two reasons—a slip in the ratings, and CBS's decision to purge itself of its old

♥ **Taking a dip in "the cement pond."**

folksy demographics and get hipper. CBS dropped *Petticoat Junction, Green Acres,* and *The Red Skelton Show.*

Ironically, CBS couldn't quite get rid of all the paperwork for *The Beverly Hillbillies.* They were still battling a lawsuit by Hamilton Morgen. Morgen had written a script called *Country Cousins,* and had given it to CBS three times, first in 1952, and last in 1961, the year before *The Beverly Hillbillies* premiered. Though Morgen filed in 1965, it was only after the show went off the air that he won a decision, receiving a cash settlement (provided he agreed not to tell anyone how much).

For some fans, losing the show was like losing millions of dollars. Even Richard

Nixon and his wife were depressed! Just before the show left the air, Nixon told Irene Ryan (Granny on the show), "We love your show. Anytime we get a chance to look at it, we do." John Wayne was a fan, making a rare cameo appearance on the show.

"After the show was canceled, I really felt down," says Donna. "It was like part of my life had ended. I didn't know what to do."

Now married to Bob Leeds, who directed several episodes of the show, she didn't want to stay home all day. In 1973 she got her real estate license. She withstood the occasional looks of incredulity when customers realized they were being squired about by Elly May Clampett. Donna would patiently point out that 50 percent of those who take a real estate broker's test fail, and that buying a house is serious business—so let's get on with it.

Periodically Donna's accepted a commercial, or a guest-starring role on a TV show. Briefly in 1978 she experimented with a career as a country singer. The late '70s could have marked a resurgence in hillbilly humor. Donna recalls, "In 1965 I was doing a show where a family of small-town folk moved into a huge mansion and became the talk of the nation. Twelve years later the same thing happened when Jimmy Carter and his family moved into the White House!"

Donna was never nominated for an Emmy, but Elly lives on in reruns. In 1981, the Clampetts had their own TV movie, *Return of the Beverly Hillbillies.* It was just like old times. The *Daily News* called it "a stupid, insipid, insulting two hours." But fans loved it. The only change in the cast was Imogene Coca replacing Irene Ryan, who died in 1973.

Every now and then Donna enjoys getting back into the spotlight, appearing at celebrity parties and benefits.

Will there be another *Hillbillies* revival? Will Donna suddenly come back as a dramatic actress? Will she make a million-dollar real estate deal?

Who knows. Donna believes in fate. "Things happen in their own good time. I don't fight life, but go with it, one step at a time."

♥ That's all folks. Donna closes the show in one of her few films, *Frankie and Johnny* with Elvis Presley.

Sally Field

GIDGET

First broadcast: September 15, 1965
Last broadcast: September 1, 1966

THE FLYING NUN

First broadcast: September 7, 1967
Last broadcast: September 18, 1970

They called her pert. She got a little older, and they called her perky. But anyone who knew Sally Field during her days as a '60s sweetheart knew the real adjective for her: perturbed.

Born in Pasadena, California, November 6, 1946, Sally was still a shy, angry, insecure teenager when she became Gidget. The show lasted one year. Trying to avoid being a has-been at twenty-one, she grabbed the next series offer she got—*The Flying Nun*. She recalls grimly, "Everybody had jokes about me, and every gag went right to my heart."

For Sally, the '60s was a bewildering decade. Then again, so were the '50s.

Her parents divorced when she was about five, and the memory of her father, in tears over losing his wife and child, still burns. Her actress mother then married tough Jock Mahoney, a stuntman who had graduated from slapstick falls in Three Stooges comedies to Hollywood Westerns. The girl, nicknamed "Doodles," didn't get along with Jock either. Jock was too strong; playfully tossing her up in the air, imposing strict discipline through rules about proper dressing and dating.

23

Her frustration was soothed by acting. The budding teen would dress up in her mother's makeup and wardrobe and "cry and scream in front of the mirror and be very sexy." Stepfather Jock achieved some fame in 1962, becoming the latest movie Tarzan. Around that time, Sally startled classmates at Birmingham High School when she gave fine performances in school productions of *The Miracle Worker* and *Suddenly Last Summer.*

After high school, Sally immediately enrolled in acting workshops at Columbia Pictures. It was there that she was discovered for *Gidget*—along with 150 other girls. She played Francine Lawrence, five foot one, dubbed "Gidget" because she was small, a cross between a "girl and a midget."

Another word might've been *gadget*. She was a perky little toy. The show's theme song had a beach boy croon "Wait'll you see my Gidget," as if she was an accessory to his surfboard. Actually, Sally didn't even know how to surf when she became Gidget. But soon she was in the midst of it, with beach pals Moon Doggie (Steven Miles), Treasure (Beverly Adams), and Siddo (Mike Nader).

On sheer personality, Sally made Gidget come to life, even though picture-perfect Sandra Dee had played the role in the 1959 movie. Gidget was actually "born" in 1957, when Frederick Kohner wrote a book about his ditsy daughter Kathy, who really was nicknamed "Gidget."

For Sally it was a thrill to be a real actress, and to have been the lucky one chosen to become a star—

but she was also suffering through the adolescent miseries of any teenage girl—feeling awkward, immature, unsophisticated, and downright dumb. She'd look in the mirror and wonder, "Why are my cheeks so round? Why is my nose so short?" As for beach fun, she remembers what it was like in real life. Goofy muscle boys would toss her into the air on a beach blanket. "I wanted to take a machine gun to all those people," she says.

There was one definite difference between Sally and Gidget. Gidget was virginal. Sally, since the age of 15, was not. At first, sex was not pleasure, just something she felt she had to do. But that

♥ **Gidget says "Hi" : the official autographed photo sent to the author and all fans.**

changed. Soon she and high school sweetheart Steve Craig were thinking about marriage.

The show lasted only thirty-two episodes, featuring some interesting guest stars—Harvey Korman, Barbara Hershey, Daniel J. Travanti, Bonnie Franklin, Michael York, and Hazel Court. When ABC thought twice about canceling it, and then canceled it anyway, thousands of young male viewers missed their favorite sweetheart—the cute, perky beach bunny who was sexy in a neat-o wholesome way. And thousands of girls missed the one person on TV with whom they could really identify.

Suddenly dumped, Sally nervously overate, adding fifteen pounds to her petite frame. Meanwhile, ABC decided that if *Gidget* wasn't worth saving, Sally Field was. Hurrying to find another vehicle for their star, they came up with *The Flying Nun*, offering her $4,000 a week. For *Gidget*, she had gotten only $450.

Hurrying to take it, Sally let herself in for misery. The show was idiotic and she knew it. From a beach bunny, she became a sitcom silly: ninety-pound Elsie Ethrington, who joins a convent in San Juan, Puerto Rico, and becomes Sister Bertrille, a nun who actually becomes airborne when the wind kicks her habit up. She was embarrassed that during the hottest protest years of the '60s, with people flying high on drugs, sex, and revolution, she was the "Flying Nun." She even sang on an album of sugary kidstuff pop tunes.

It might've helped if the nun got married—as Sally did in real life. She married Steve Craig in 1968. In 1969 TV's nun became noticeably pregnant. "It should have been the most treasured time in my life, but there I was worrying about how tight I should pull the belt on my nun's habit."

After *The Flying Nun*, Sally tried to make her career fly. She made TV movies from 1970 to 1972 (comedies and dramas including *Maybe I'll Come Home in the Spring; Marriage: Year One; Mongo's Back in Town; Hitched;* and *Home for the Holidays*). She had a second son in 1972.

Supporting her husband (a writer who was still taking courses in college) and two kids, Sally decided she had to become Sally Burton in *The Girl with Something Extra*, a 1973 sitcom with John Davidson as her newlywed hubby. In a variation on *Bewitched*, she had some powers—ESP—but not enough for the show to stay on the air.

Sick of sitcoms, disillusioned, Sally "changed everything at once—I got rid of my agent, my business manager, my house, and my husband." She adds, "My anger at everything—the responsibility of raising two children, the hiding of who I am, the limping in front of the lame, the compromises within my own home and in my work—came bubbling out. I was reaching the point where I wanted to pursue my dreams."

Sally studied acting—seriously—with Lee Strasberg. She was hungry for a good role, and when the movie *Stay Hungry* came along, she went for it. When the director met with her, and questioned if she could play the sexy lead role, she startled him by saying, "I'm the best fuck in town!"

Stay Hungry got her good notices. Strangely, when it came time to cast the TV movie *Sybil*, it wasn't a Hollywood producer who picked her for the part. It was . . . Sybil herself. As Sally says, "For her to pick me, and for me to actually get it, is bizarre. Correct me if I'm wrong."

In *Sybil* she played a woman with a slight personality problem—sixteen different identities. Sally worked all her fears, passions, rages, and pains into that role, and she won an Emmy. She didn't attend the ceremony though. She was home with her new lover, Burt Reynolds.

Having Burt around changed Sally tremendously. If he thought she was sexy, then she *was*. With some trepidations, she let him cast her in *Smokey and the Bandit*. Only *Star Wars* grossed more money that year. Burt and Sally appeared in a few more films together, including *The End* and *Hooper*, and then she stepped over the line of commerciality with *Beyond the Poseidon Adventure*. This was a disaster movie, literally: "It was God's way of giving me one final kick in the behind. I'll never do anything like it again." Sally was getting edgy for a change.

She swapped lighthearted romances for *Norma Rae*, and her powerful portrayal of a union organizer proved that her brilliance in *Sybil* was no fluke. Sally became, in a *U.S. News & World Report* poll, one of America's ten most respected people. She won an Academy Award. A shocked Sally told the crowd, "I'm going to be the one to cry tonight, I'll tell you that right now. They said this couldn't be done." Then, after thanking the people behind the camera, she thanked her two sons. "If it weren't for them I wouldn't be worth a damn."

Backstage, cooled down, she still wondered about her worth. "I do feel like the Academy is slacking off in the class quotient," she told reporters. "After all—I won."

Critics were beginning to appreciate her, at least most of them. Vincent Canby of *The New York Times* noted, "I certainly don't agree with a friend of mine who says that Miss Field is simply a Mary Tyler Moore someone has stepped on."

Conspicuously absent on awards night was Burt Reynolds, chagrined that he hadn't been nominated for his own breakthrough, *Starting Over*. A maverick about award shows anyway, he recalls, "I sat home alone like a wounded Citizen Kane, visualizing Sally dancing with Dustin Hoffman at the Academy ball."

The relationship between Burt and Sally was eroding.

As with previous sweetheart Judy Carne, Burt had been trying to make over Sally Field. He wanted her to dress a certain way and act a certain way. For five years, Sally had enjoyed his approval. She enjoyed being the sexy, glamorous lover to Hollywood's number-one male sex symbol. And for Sally, Burt balanced macho with humor and a great deal of warmth. But, as she later admitted during a *Playboy* interview, the role-playing could last only so long. "I got mad. And

♥ **Sally turns sexy—with Burt Reynolds encouraging her, she goes for the glamour. A scene from *The End*.**

all the colors that I try to hide from all these guys—these fathers and men—finally came out. I mean, it was Sybil: 'This won't do, that won't do, I don't like it' . . . What the fuck is going on? I am a human and these are my needs and how do they fit in with yours?"

The bewildered Burt couldn't figure it out. Part of the problem was that neither could Sally, who was only beginning to work out her emotional needs and anger. After the *Playboy* interview, the saga of Sally and Burt was in all the tabloids. The *Star* blazed a headline: "Why I left Burt Reynolds . . . I stopped existing . . . I

dressed for him . . . I walked for him . . . I was so dependent."

Asked for his side of the story, Burt told *US* magazine, "I'm not going to get in a urinating contest with Sally because I'd lose."

That fascinating imagery aside, he did refute her claim that he begged her to marry him: "I'm good at some things, but begging ain't one of them. There was a time when I thought we were going to get married, but for some reason we didn't." He prided himself that he had pushed for Sally to be in *Smokey and the Bandit* when Universal Studios had little faith in her sex appeal. And he searched his memory but could not remember manipulating her, or forcing her to make more films with him. In fact, he couldn't even remember being *that* serious about her, since they never lived together—they both had separate homes, and Sally was often at hers taking care of the kids.

After the breakup, Sally, who had really not had many men in her life—she had gone almost directly from her high school sweetheart–first husband to Burt Reynolds—was seen in the company of quite a few eligible bachelors, including Johnny Carson and Kevin Kline. "I know much more about myself as an actor than I do as a partner to a man," she once told *Playboy*. "I've just started to learn about that. Once you make love with someone and you decide to love him, it's the start of all sorts of things you didn't really know were there—really starting to learn how to make love. Making love with strangers is not making love, because

27

you don't love them. It's called fucking."

In 1984 she married producer Alan Greisman. The marriage ceremony was nonsectarian. A few years later she admitted, "I don't know that I've ever really fallen in love with anybody. I've fallen deeply into infatuation, and deeply into like, and fallen deeply into want— whether it was sexual want or my want for someone to be important, or my want that I be important to him. Even my husband . . . I don't think I fell in love with him. I am learning now to love him. It was the

♥ **An early attempt at dropping the *Flying Nun* sitcom sweetie image: playing a hooker in *Back Roads*.**

most adult thing that I think I've ever done."

Sally had made several important films in the early '80s, playing tough and challenging parts as a whore *(Back Roads)* and as an unsympathetic, overtly feminist reporter *(Absence of Malice)*. Film fans were used to the new Sally Field, but not blasé enough to overlook her exceptional performance in 1984's *Places in the Heart*. She won an Oscar for the second time. Of that emotional movie, Sally recalls, "Playing Edna Spalding opened me up. I rediscovered that people are meant to need each other."

Director Robert Benton enthused, "Sally Field is a total actress . . . she has that combination of intelligence and instinct . . . she has the courage to risk anything . . . most actresses hide behind something. They hide behind a technique. They hide behind a trick . . ." But on the set, Sally's emotions were genuine. And she gave it all she had, take after take, never complaining.

Almost as dramatic as the movie itself was Sally's appearance on the Academy Awards telecast, March 25, 1985. Determined to be in touch with her feelings, buoyed by the excitement of the moment, she gave a heartfelt acceptance speech. "This means so much more to me this time, I don't know why. I think the first time I hardly felt it because it was all too new." Looking out at the glittering movie stars, the ex-TV queen continued, "I haven't had an orthodox career and I wanted more than anything to have your respect. The first time I didn't feel it, but this time I feel it." Her voice rising, Sally cried, "I can't deny the fact—that you like me—right now you like me!"

The crowd exploded in applause and laughter. They seemed to appreciate Sally's almost childlike ability to let her emotions show. But afterward, many seemed to be thinking, "Oh, grow up!" *USA Today* booed her "I'm OK—you're OK" acceptance speech, and standup comics had a field day doing jokes that ended, "You like me! You really like me!"

Even Burt Reynolds dropped it, if unintentionally. After the *Playboy* piece, a still-bitter Burt complained to an interviewer, "I thought she liked me."

To ensure that she would continue to appear in worthy films, Sally formed her own production company. Sally, like Goldie Hawn, realized that the best way of ensuring good roles in worthy pictures was to find them herself. As she told writer Jonathan Black, "To get ahead in a man's world you've got to have drive. You better be the first one there. You better be the one to push your way in that door. I love ambition. Any time I've ever been attracted to a man he's always been very ambitious. Ambition is very attractive. But, but—I do think you have to constantly keep it in check. I've seen plenty of people who are more ambitious than talented or sensitive, and it's a very irritating combination. It can also be dangerous."

The first film she worked on as a producer was *Home Before Morning*, about a nurse during the Vietnam War. A script was written, revised, and ultimately re-

♥ They like her and she knows it! An Oscar winner for *Places in the Heart.*

jected. Instead, she did *Murphy's Romance*, a romantic comedy with James Garner. It was a hit. Rex Reed wrote, "Sally Field continues to be one of the screen's most natural and engaging actresses, and it's a treat to see her in a role for a change that doesn't place the burdens of the world on her tiny but shapely shoulders."

The following year, she was opposite Michael Caine in *Surrender*. The characters meet rather strangely—during a robbery, thieves strip them and tie them up together. After this, Michael wants to raise Cain. Says Sally, "I make it a policy never to have sex before the first date."

29

She felt enough distance had passed from her TV sitcom years to mix drama with comedy in 1988's *Punchline*. When *Punchline* ended filming, the forty-year-old actress was expecting a baby. Her other children, Eli and Peter, were fifteen and eighteen. "I just sat down and started to cry. Because I know the kind of commitment it means . . . it's scary to think that there will be another human being in the world that I will love that much. It's like, oh my God, do I want to feel this . . . this much again?"

She told *Parade* magazine, "You know, you feel like all those clichés about motherhood—I am godlike, that I'm able to do this." Sally maintains a very secure home life; taking the kids to school, spending ninety minutes each morning doing Jane Fonda workouts. If she's not filming, she's supervising details at her production company. And since she has no cook or maid, there are cooking and cleaning chores to share too.

In her public life, Sally is still committed to the ungodlike world of politics. After having supported Gary Hart (along with Goldie Hawn), she turned her attentions to a new candidate in the 1988 race, Michael Dukakis, announcing, "We need him, America needs him." But she didn't say "really."

Of all the sweethearts of the '60s, Sally has probably put the most distance between her TV roles and her movie roles. *Gidget* is not widely syndicated. *The Flying Nun* is around, but as much a silly joke now as it was then. On the other hand, people continue to purchase videos of *Norma Rae* and *Places in the Heart*.

How does Sally feel about watching those old sitcoms? "My God," she says, "why doesn't someone put a bag over her head and cart her off?"

Marlo Thomas

THAT GIRL

First broadcast: September 8, 1966
Last broadcast: September 10, 1971

Cute little button nose. Cheerful outlook. Fresh face. Ann Marie was the kind of girl to take kite flying. To the zoo. But not to bed! What would happen if she was asked? Probably her wide, innocent eyes would roll. Her voice would turn into a throaty squeak. And she'd utter a gasp of disapproval: "Ohhhh, Dawwwwnald!"

As "That Girl," Marlo Thomas was the ultimate in princess girlfriends, the kind to be placed on a pedestal and pecked on the cheek. She was the dream "nice girl" that every boy's mom hoped he'd find one day. As a sitcom, *That Girl* was light-hearted good clean fun. And as Ann Marie, Marlo Thomas played it to perfection.

How close was Ann Marie to the real Marlo?

"I was much more serious than 'That Girl,'" Marlo recalls now. "But, in a way, that kind of 'Oh boy golly geewhiz we have an easy solution to everything' was what I thought you were supposed to do. I thought it was the right way to take on life, with a tremendous amount of optimism. The only bad thing about optimism is that it can start to mask problems—and you can't be optimistic forever if you don't solve your problems."

Marlo had to solve some problems early, foremost being that she was the daughter of a celebrity, Danny Thomas. Half Lebanese and half Italian, Margaret Julia Thomas was born in Detroit on November 21, 1938 (some sources make it 1943). Her early years were marked by constant, disorienting travel, as Danny played club after club. When the singer bought the family a home, he still was never there. He stopped the touring when Marlo said stop. She was in seventh grade, and wrote a school paper called "Viva Today." Danny was making plenty of bucks preparing for the future—but, she asked, where was he today?

Danny found a solution—stay home and do a TV series. Marlo was happy—except when she watched *Make Room for Daddy* and saw her father cuddling his make-believe daughter.

Thomas sent Marlo to Catholic school, where his own strict and conservative ideas were amplified by the nuns. "Back when I was a teenage girl, I thought teenage boys were really dangerous. Everybody said they were. The nuns who were my teachers said they were. They said you shouldn't sit on a boy's lap without putting a newspaper or a pillow down first.

"They said you shouldn't wear patent-leather shoes because your underpants would be reflected in them. I'm not kidding, that's exactly what they said. Ask any woman who went to Catholic school.

"I wish somebody had told me in high school how vulnerable teenage boys were. I thought they had it all under control—'Mr. Cool'—but they're just like we are. Just as nervous as we were as young girls."

The guys Marlo dated had to be nervous; when they brought her back from a date, they had to face Danny, and he was usually armed with a shotgun! "I knew he was just into his Daddy role with a vengeance," Marlo recalls, "and that he wasn't going to shoot anybody, but there were some poor guys I never heard from again. Who could blame them?"

Marlo couldn't really get mad at her father, whose stern ways were often marked by such sitcom exaggeration. The Thomas family enjoyed robust meals, good times, and a lot of joking. Though a disciplinarian, Danny was fair, always careful to explain his decisions, which Marlo appreciated.

Marlo went to the University of Southern California (Danny insisted she stay close to home) and graduated summa cum laude. An English major, she had offers for a teaching career. Instead, she decided to go to New York and become an actress.

Like the dour but loving Mr. Marie on *That Girl*, Danny disliked having his daughter living alone in the big city. They got into a shouting match and she walked out. They made up—after Marlo got to New York.

A feminist before there was such a term, when Marlo had the chance to star in her own sitcom she decided it should be about a woman on her own. On first glance, *That Girl* doesn't seem exactly feminist, but in its cute little sitcom way, it was. This unmarried ex-suburbanite from Brewster, New York, wanted a career, and her own apartment. It wasn't *Sex and the Single Girl*, since she was seeing a near-nebbish guy named Donald Hol-

♥ "That Girl" was everybody's pinup sweetheart. Autographed photo sent to the author.

linger (Ted Bessell), but it was at least "the single girl."

Marlo was cute—her tiny nose and pale lipstick accentuated her big, bright eyes. She had a charmingly squeaky voice, like a little girl. With her modest, trimly girlish physique, she looked adorable in the doll-like clothes designed by Suzanne Smith. The theme song (the lyrics were added a few years later) characterized her this way: "Diamonds, daisies, snowflakes! That Girl! Chestnuts, rain-

bows, springtime . . . That Girl!" The chorus hinted, "If you find a girl to love, only one girl to love, then she'll be That Girl too."

That Marlo could keep the show sweet without being saccharine, charmingly coy without being cloying, is a tribute to the personality and human believability she brought to the role.

There was only the gentlest bit of suggestiveness on the show, the program's morality being slightly to the right of the pious Danny Thomas himself. In one episode, would-be actress Ann Marie discovers that a movie part requires a nude scene. She has doubts, especially reading the script to Donald:

Ann: "Angela walks into the room . . . she is . . ."

Don: "She is what?"

Ann: "Uh, she's ummmm—"

Don: "What? Mad?"

Ann: "Ummm . . ."

Don: "Laughing?"

Ann: "She is . . ."

Don: "What! *What!* What?"

Squeaky whisper from Ann: "Naked!"

This was adorable, at least for a few years, those years before the publication of books like *Nice Girls Do*.

Naïve, romantic young men went steady with "That Girl" through to the end of the '60s, and virginal girls dreamed about having the keen life that Ann Marie had, with her zany neighbors, acting auditions, own apartment, fun clothes—and friendly "boyfriend" (as opposed to scary "lover").

Ann had lots of fun pals—a cast that included Dabney Coleman as a next-door neighbor, George Carlin as an agent, and Ruth Buzzi as a friend. She lived at 627 East Fifty-fourth, which, if such a number existed, would have put her in the middle of the East River. But this was the unsinkable Ann Marie. Even now, reruns of *That Girl* help buoy old-fashioned virtues, at least to young children watching, and rekindle a certain childlike spirit and zest in older fans.

One late episode featured a guest appearance by Danny Thomas, handled absolutely straight:

"You're Danny Thomas!" shouts Ann Marie.

"Yes, I know."

"Oh my gosh, Mr. Thomas, I've been a fan of yours for years!"

Ann Marie gets quite a treat when, at a Friar's Club dinner, she gets the chance to do a comedy routine with Milton Berle and then sing a duet with Danny.

As the '60s petered out, so did the show. *That Girl* was a sweet fantasy, but

♥ **Postcard sent to the author announcing Marlo's "new image" on the show for 1970.**

See "That Girl" at a new time with her new look.

Marlo 1969

Marlo 1970

Marlo was no longer a girl. The '70s started with cosmetic changes updating Ann Marie. She got a new hairstyle and almost grew into "That Woman," as Donald proposed marriage. But that little plot twist didn't help a show that, like a kite, had begun to crash to earth under the naïve supposition that fluffy white clouds and a gentle breeze would always be enough.

Marlo lost her one *That Girl* Emmy nomination to Lucille Ball, but with 136 episodes of *That Girl* in the can, she became, like Lucy, a rerun favorite. She didn't need to go right into another sitcom. Money was no problem—Danny Thomas had taught her the business well, and *That Girl* paid handsome residuals. She became involved in a variety of projects; marches, demonstrations, feminist crusades.

At one lecture, a man stood up and said, "What do you think about . . . an old-fashioned girl who will cook . . . clean . . . call him the boss . . . and be waiting with a martini when he gets home from work?"

Marlo asked, "Can you find this girl?"

He said, "I have!"

She said, "Well, then, by all means, marry her." Then she added, "Just be sure to enjoy it while you can, because in five years she could be one angry woman."

Intelligent, sensitive, able to explain emotions and feelings well, Marlo could expound on feminist themes without becoming strident or seeming bitter. She found a ready audience on talk shows.

Her father told her, "My only discomfort about your life is that I've always prayed and hoped that a strong man would be at your side, to protect you and keep you company, help you raise your children. A lifelong mate to hold your hand. That person you can turn your back on and know you won't get kicked, who loves your neck and your back and your feet, who feeds you chicken soup . . ."

In 1974 Marlo became a sweetheart of the '70s—to children. As a sweetheart of the '60s she'd given kids a live version of what their Ken and Barbie dolls might be like living in the big city as boyfriend and girlfriend, and what it would be like if they could grow up in the nice, cute world of Ann and Donald. In the book and record *Free to Be You and Me*, she and her celebrity friends offered lessons in independence and nonsexist friendship.

In 1977 Marlo costarred with Wayne Rogers in *It Happened One Christmas*, a TV movie based on *It's a Wonderful Life*. She longed for weightier dramas, and after sweating out acting classes with Lee Strasberg, was able to make it to serious made-for-TV dramas. She starred in *Consenting Adult*, playing the mother of a gay son. She starred in *The Lost Honor of Kathryn Beck*, based on a novel by Heinrich Böll; *The Lost Honor of Katharina Blum*.

After that, she took some time off for something a bit lighter. She won good notices for her Broadway show *Social Security*. Recalling the story line, she says the play was "about sex, and money, and sex."

Sex was not something one thought of in relation to the pure and adorable Ann

Marie. But now that she was really Marlo Thomas, reporters were curious about her. The reason was her choice of lovers—Phil Donahue. They'd met when Marlo guested on his Chicago show in 1976, promoting *Thieves*. The 1977 film had won some nice notices. "Marlo Thomas is completely enchanting," wrote Judith Crist in *Saturday Review*.

For Marlo, Phil Donahue was completely enchanting: "He walked into the green room and I tell you, my little heart stopped beating!" she laughs. Aside from his looks, what impressed her was that he asked her questions about her mother, not Danny Thomas. A man interested in the problem of mother-daughter relationships? Marlo melted—as everyone watching the show could see.

"It's so embarrassing," Marlo says with a smile. Her infatuation with Phil "was so obvious." Her voice crawled up to the same hoarse squeak of "That Girl." Only instead of "Dawwwnald!" it was "Oh! Phil!"

She said to him, "You are loving and generous and you like women. It's a pleasure and whoever the woman in your life is she's very lucky."

And suddenly Phil's questions became as squoshy as Marlo's answers. "What sort of men do you date?" he asked. After the show, they were both tingling with excitement. Phil managed to drop in when she did a TV interview at another show. He asked his pals if she liked him. She wondered if he had as much of a crush on her as she had on him. Phil promised to look her up when he came to Los An-

geles. On their first date, she dressed up in the sexiest outfit she could find, a slinky number in jet black. The sensitive talk-show host thought she looked like Spiderwoman. Even so, that one date turned into three years of dating.

At first, neither was interested in marriage. Marlo had avoided marriage for two decades. Her mother's lack of fulfillment was the main reason. Her mother had given up her singing career to marry Danny and have kids. In fact, Marlo's insistence on a career, and *That Girl*, was, in her words, "mother's revenge." And so the career dominated, and marriage was not considered. Even after so many years, Marlo wanted to avoid the possibility of being dominated by a partner. Phil had already been married and divorced, and had five kids.

After much discussion, they were married on May 22, 1980.

Some feminist reporters were dismayed. Writer Susie Dworkin noted that Marlo "was the queen of the single girls" who had been "the ego ideal of women who did not get married young." She asked why Marlo got married. Dworkin recalls, "She looked me in the eye and said, 'If I asked you why you married your husband, what would you answer?'"

The married writer answered, "I loved him. I didn't want to be without him. I wanted to make a special commitment to him, above all others."

Marlo laughed and said, "That's it. You got it."

She admitted that "For me to even want to marry, the rules had to change, the whole society had to change. And those changes have had to do with the independence, the quality of women within the marriage. And of course, I had to meet a man who had changed too."

Marlo was asked her opinion of marriage. "Marriage had a bad name in my book," she said. "It used to be mud, now I'm willing to call it cloudy water . . . Phil is the greatest husband in the world and he's nothing to brag about."

She's changed her mind since. "I used to believe that sex would grow less interesting as one grew older." But no, she officially stopped thinking that way "on my last birthday."

On Phil's fiftieth birthday, she sang a song to him: "He's just my Phil, with twenty pounds of hair. He'd have to get a trim before you'd notice him. An Irish hunk, so full of spunk. A Rock of Gibraltar inside of an altar boy. I gladly share with women everywhere their daily thrill. 'Cause later when he comes home to me—I know he's just my Phil."

At forty-eight, Marlo has found her home life as much of a priority as her work. She doesn't simply take acting roles to "keep busy." When "reunion fever" began in 1985, and TV movies based on *Perry Mason, I Dream of Jeannie,* and *The Andy Griffith Show* surfaced, there was some talk of *That Girl* being updated. Ted Bessell was still around—a director now with a wife and two kids. But Marlo wasn't interested. "I grew up," she told the audience at the *Sally Jessy Raphael Show.* "*That Girl* is now *Cagney and Lacey* and *Kate and Allie.*"

♥ A real "new image"—Marlo wins an Emmy for her brilliant dramatic role in *Nobody's Child.*

In 1986, she chose one of her most impressive acting assignments yet, one that has won her critical acclaim. She played Marie Balter in the TV movie *Nobody's Child.* Balter wasn't "That Girl," she was an abused girl—traumatized by her adoptive mother.

"She was locked out. Her parents locked her out of her house at five years old. She was struggling to belong and I think it's a very universal feeling that we all have. We all feel locked out of someplace, we're all struggling through our work, through our love life, through whatever, our struggle all our lives is to belong somewhere, and she survived it."

Marlo told *TV Guide* that Marie "suffered from endogenous depression and panic disorder. Endogenous means that the depression comes from within and has no apparent cause. Panic disorder means that the panic hits without warning, and you get so scared your throat closes, you can't breathe, you feel like you're going to die . . . to enter Marie's mind, I had to face up to the forces that make me panic, and then play them to myself, and turn the volume up and up and up."

Balter endured electroshock treatments, straitjackets, and drugs—before fighting her way back to freedom. She married, earned a degree at Harvard, and became a leading spokeswoman for mental health care. But it took twenty years of emotional hell. It seemed to take as long for Marlo to film the role. She spent hours and hours learning to walk with a stagger, taping her fingers together to experience helpless sensations, calling up images of herself as a child and the times she visited a relative who had suffered from mental illness.

As she told NBC's Jack Cafferty, her home life with Donahue wasn't much fun: "Phil kept saying, 'I can't wait till the movie is over' because I had nightmares from it. We all have a little damaged child inside of us. Adulthood is about healing that child—that's the real victory of growing up, that you take care of that little child who didn't get taken care of in some way. And no matter how great your childhood was I think all human beings have

something they didn't get. Some approval, some love, something they didn't get and we struggle all our lives to fill that hole."

Marlo got approval in review after review. Jennifer Regan in the *New York Post* wrote, "Thomas's portrait as she struggles out of depression and actual physical regression—at one point she can't walk or feed herself for two years—is believable to a fault. Her face, by turns haggard and hopeful, and physical movements register every step forward and every setback as she exchanges a dependence in institutional life for the child-like wonder of an adult emerging into reality . . ."

Marlo met with Marie Balter several times. "I think it's the most intimate I ever felt with any part I've ever played, and I think a lot of that is Marie herself, the extraordinary woman she is."

Marlo says the role "was scary because you have to dig very far to find the demons in yourself and face the things that frighten you most. But it's worth it because once you do—once you understand somebody else's journey—it helps you with your own." Marlo won an Emmy for *Nobody's Child*, her fourth win out of seven nominations.

Making the movie was a courageous move, but just one of the many she made in the years since *That Girl*. Lately she's again turned her attention to children. She's become a sweetheart of the '80s to them, via *Free to Be . . . a Family*, a book (and record) aimed at six-to-twelve-year-olds about love and belonging.

Asked for her thoughts on courage for

the inspirational book *Courage Is a Three-Letter Word*, Marlo said, "Courage is doing it anyway, whatever *it* is. We all doubt ourselves . . . we all wonder whether we really have the goods."

Marlo's thoughtful comments have often been quoted. She even won a page in a *365 Quotes a Day* calendar for 1988: "Never face facts; if you do, you'll never get up in the morning." She elaborates: "When we line up all the facts that we believe are against us, the facts can stop us before we start. Whatever we need to discourage us—'I'm too young, too old, too short, too tall, unprepared, inexperienced, or not quite ready'—we can uncover. And if we miss a few details, we can always find someone to help us 'face the facts.' The facts, after all, speak for themselves—except they're not true."

Marlo has truly not let herself be stopped. For Marlo Thomas, *That Girl* is way in the past. She's "That Woman," with an unlimited future. To borrow from Phil Donahue's introduction when she appeared on his show for the first time in eleven years, she's "always beautiful, ever popular, eternally creative . . ."

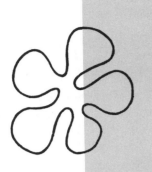

Dream Wives

Mary Tyler Moore

THE DICK VAN DYKE SHOW

First broadcast: October 3, 1961
Last broadcast: September 7, 1966

Newsweek got it right, way back in 1966: "Mary Tyler Moore is more than the girl next door—she is the fantasy girl of the American Dream."

For five years, she costarred on *The Dick Van Dyke Show*, one of the very first sitcoms for adults. But kids were watching too. If girls still thought they were going to grow up to be housewives, Laura Petrie was the one they wanted to be. She was pretty. She had a dancer's elegance. She had fun. She wore her hair like Jackie Kennedy (and Dick Van Dyke was sort of John F. Kennedy).

Boys? The younger ones had to envy dopey Little Richie, who got a chance to snuggle close to Mary every week. The older ones wanted a wife like Laura Petrie—the only TV housewife with sex appeal. Donna Reed didn't wear capri pants, did she?

As Laura Petrie, Mary Tyler Moore was the closest thing '60s television had to a flesh-and-blood wife. Despite the constraints of sitcom reality, Laura was real. Sitcom silly but emotional, sitcom conservative but impish, a sitcom "happy housewife" and "mom" who could purr, "I'm a woman," and saunter into the bedroom (as she did in the very first episode), Mary, as Laura, left no doubt that *this* sitcom couple was having fun in bed. Even

♥ Looking cute and timid, or just plain uneasy—Mary poses for an early publicity shot.

mits, "I think a lot of my career drive is based on a childhood need to get Daddy's approval and attention."

She showed off as a ballerina, and dreamed of becoming a movie star. When the family moved to California, she knew she was moving closer to that dream. Her idol was Leslie Caron: "Caron had all those teeth, and I was so self-conscious about my big mouth. But there she was, adored for her big mouth, plus she was a brilliant dancer."

Mary was a good dancer, but not brilliant. In Catholic schools she was a "lousy" student, more interested in boys. Despite stern disapproval from the nuns, she didn't stay with the other girls when there were boys at the playground. In high school she dated quite a bit, and was frustrated by the restrictions placed on "good girls." As she says, "I was a very good Catholic girl. I was a virgin when I married, but I knew when I was dating that there were too many restrictions placed on you, too many sexual taboos."

At seventeen, Mary began seeing twenty-seven-year-old Richard Meeker, a man of the world with manly hobbies like gun collecting. They married in 1955. At home she was Mrs. Meeker, but TV viewers knew her as "Happy Hotpoint," the Peter Pan—like femlin who appeared in commercials on *Ozzie and Harriet*, shouting "Hi, Harriet, aren't you glad that you own a Hotpoint refrigerator?"

Mary Tyler Moore (she was originally

if they had to push those long-distance twin beds together to do it.

Mary was unpredictable, herself. All through her Catholic school—dominated childhood, she teeter-tottered between conservative obedience and curiosity-filled naughtiness. She was born on December 29, 1937, in Brooklyn. Her father was an enigmatic, distant man, with a dull job at a local utility company. Mr. Moore had little time for Mary. She ad-

44

just Mary Moore, but used the middle name to avoid confusion with actress Terry Moore) was getting big. Her figure blossomed to an enticing 36-24-36. But then it went to 36-26-36. And 36-28-36. Pregnant, she lost the part of "Happy Hotpoint." After her son Richard was born, in July of 1956, Mary returned to her career. Even her husband realized that she was unhappy as a housewife—a mediocre cook and totally unfulfilled by keeping house.

Mary's dancing was good enough to get her work in the chorus lines of various TV variety shows. In 1957, her dancer's legs won her the part of "Sam" on *Richard Diamond, Private Detective*, a crime show starring David Janssen. All the audience saw was her legs! The camera stayed on those flexing legs while she answered the phone as Diamond's secretary. "I spoke in a very low sexy voice," says Mary. "I don't do that anymore."

Mary wasn't expecting too much out of the show, but the quirky idea of a sexy secretary, all purring voice and long legs, intrigued viewers. Who *was* this mystery girl? *TV Guide* grabbed Mary, handed her a bunch of stockings, and did a photo shoot: "Sam Models the Latest in Hosiery." In thirteen weeks, Mary was a leggy legend.

Naturally, Mary asked for a raise. When she didn't get it, she left the show. She began making the rounds of the other detective shows, like *77 Sunset Strip* and *Hawaiian Eye*, usually playing sexy-but-nice sweethearts. She auditioned for Sherry Jackson's role on Danny Thomas's

Make Room for Daddy. Danny liked the sweet, unpretentious Mary, but insisted, "Nobody could believe that a daughter like mine would have a nose like yours!"

In 1961, Mary was still nosing around for something good when *The Dick Van Dyke Show* began casting. Finding the right match for Dick Van Dyke was tough. "We've run out of prospects," someone told producer Danny Thomas. "Can you think of more?"

Moore?

Danny remembered. She was called—but having been so rarely chosen, she came to the audition without much enthusiasm. To producer Carl Reiner, she simply read her audition lines as herself. She said: "Hello, Rob, are you home?"

Reiner went crazy: "I grabbed her by the hair . . . she thought I was going to rape her . . ." He told everyone he had found just what he was looking for, a girl who said "hello" just like "a real person."

The Dick Van Dyke Show was about real people. It was based on Carl Reiner's life as a comedy writer living in the suburbs. In fact, Reiner had done the pilot himself with Barbara Britton as his wife. To help the show ring true, there was no canned laugh track—the show was filmed in front of an audience, almost like a play. That was only one of many innovations on this pioneering show.

Doing comedy for the first time, Mary had to grow into the part. At first, the doings at 448 Bonnie Meadow Road in New Rochelle were only slightly less contrived than other sitcoms. Laura Petrie was, in

♥ **The ultimate housewife, '60s style. Laura and Rob Petrie in suburbia.**

her own words, "a nag." In early episodes she made husband Rob leave a party and come rushing home because of her (faulty) premonition that Little Richie was sick. She got ridiculously jealous over other women. She was even a snoop, opening up her husband's mail. Flashback tales of how Rob and Laura met when she was a USO dancer were also unflattering—she seemed petulant and distant, almost a self-absorbed princess.

Gradually, the sitcom Laura disappeared, and the "real" Mary Tyler Moore–influenced Laura came out. Mary enjoyed wearing capri pants at home. She reasoned that Laura Petrie would, too. Besides, wearing a dress to do housework

was just plain dumb. Suddenly—there was Laura Petrie, the first TV housewife in pants!

The sponsors were very concerned about this. Carl Reiner was told that Mary's bottom was, well, "sculptured too well." The "undercupping" was too revealing! She was told to wear dresses—but when viewer mail was solidly behind the pants, Laura Petri was once more at ease in those capris.

Along with the sexy physical changes Mary brought to the role of housewife, the scripts began to accentuate character over stunt comedy. If Mary got into Lucille Ball-ish situations—dyeing her hair blond, getting her toe stuck in a bathtub faucet—she handled them with a charmingly authentic fluster, not a pratfall. Rob Petrie married a woman, not a clown.

Laura-watchers loved the episode where a mad painter (Carl Reiner) displayed a nude painting of her—having filled in with his imagination a lot more than she had stood (or sat) for. Then there was the "nightmare" episode where she was a sexy alien from Twylo, who kept walnuts in her closet and an extra pair of eyes in back of her head. And then there was the dream episode where she played a dance-hall hostess, singing a rousing chorus of "I don't care!"

Like housewives around the country just beginning to stand up for themselves, Laura was a bit timid at first. Her version of the Stan Laurel cry technique was a squeaky "Ohhhh Rob!" Later, she'd venture a witty comeback—learning to overcome her fears. In one memorable episode Laura nervously appears on a talk show and blurts out that Rob's boss, TV star Alan Brady, wears a toupee. Literally called on the carpet, she timidly endures the boss's ire. Brady fumes, "What do you suggest I do with all these toupees, now!" She answers pluckily, "Well, Alan, there must be some needy bald people . . ."

Laura was no dummy. Once she came to Rob's office to fill in for the secretary—and ended up helping with the jokes. She was no pushover, either. In another episode she demonstrated a Judo move—that flipped Rob right on his back, severely bruising his ego.

Relations on the set were always cordial. Most coworkers remember Mary as efficient and somewhat distant. She only had one temper tantrum—she walked off the set during the filming of the toe-in-the-faucet episode, annoyed that she was going to be off-camera for most of the show. Ten minutes of sulking, and she was in the bathtub, soaking.

Mary was nominated for an Emmy in 1963, losing to Shirley Booth for *Hazel*. In 1964 she won, beating out Booth, Patty Duke, Inger Stevens, and Irene Ryan. She won again in 1965, beating Lucille Ball and Elizabeth Montgomery. It looked like she would go on winning, but Dick Van Dyke and Carl Reiner knew it was better to quit while they were ahead. They decided not to go back into production.

When the show died, Mary cried. "I was heartbroken. I wanted it to go on forever."

Nothing lasted forever. Her marriage had ended just as *The Dick Van Dyke Show* became successful in 1962. She insists the problem was not her stardom, or her hectic schedule, but basic incompatibility. Over the years, young Mary had matured. Meeker, ten years older, had remained the same. For example, he still loved his guns. Mary had become a supporter of animal rights; she was disgusted by hunting.

Later during the *Van Dyke Show* run, Mary was introduced to an advertising exec. He asked her for a date almost immediately. Did he think he could use her so easily? Instead of just saying no, she decided to teach *him* a lesson. He'd have to take her out to the hottest show in town (Broadway's *Mary Mary*) and to a hot nightspot (the Peppermint Lounge). And then? Good-bye, Mr. Chump!

But this ad exec, Grant Tinker, had more than superficial charm and good looks. As Mary put it, "I woke up the next morning and knew I was in love."

Like her first husband, Grant was a decade older than Mary, leading amateur psychologists to conclude she was still hung-up on her father, that unsupportive and distant figure from her childhood. Her "hang-up" with fatherly Grant Tinker lasted a good long time.

After the *Van Dyke Show*, Mary was still a '60s sweetheart. Her movie roles in 1966 and 1967 were bland "good girl" parts. She costarred with Julie Andrews in *Thoroughly Modern Millie*, costarred with a toucan in *What's So Bad About Feeling Good?*, and played opposite Robert Wagner in *Don't Just Stand There*. She closed out the decade with a horrendous Broadway flop musical version of *Breakfast at Tiffany's*, and a dopey Elvis Presley film, *Change of Habit* (Ed Asner had a supporting role). Playing a nun in this 1969 film, Mary reached the end of the decade and nearly the end of her film career. The film is now considered a "Golden Turkey." Bad film buffs Harry and Michael Medved skewered her Doris Day–like role of the ultimate "attractive virgin," and wondered about a film where only attempted rape—and Elvis Presley—can change a nun's habits.

Mary's private life was going even worse than her career.

She and Grant hoped to have a child, but she suffered a miscarriage. Devastated, the doctors gave her more bad news. They discovered that she was a diabetic, and that meant daily insulin injections.

It had been all downhill after *The Dick Van Dyke Show*. The late '60s hadn't been much better for Dick Van Dyke, who also made some career-stalling films. In 1969, he and Mary came back to the small screen for a TV special, *Dick Van Dyke and the Other Woman*. Viewers loved it. They wanted them back on TV where they belonged.

The special springboarded both into new series. Dick's was a fairly standard husband-and-wife sitcom that didn't make it. It was too '60s for the '70s. Mary's was about a single career woman, a person trying to "make it" despite her own little insecurities and flaws, without the perfection of suburban marital bliss.

As Mary said, "I play me. I'm scared that if I tamper with it, I might ruin it. My forte is not being funny, but reacting in a funny way to those around me." True, she did swap her "Oh Rob!" for a similar wail—"Oh, Mr. Grant"—but that was only natural; the show was true to the spirit of her old series, with its adult approach and emphasis on human frailties and follies.

Mary's show premiered September 19, 1970. There were some early stumbling moments. Ted Bessell, of *That Girl*, was an early boyfriend. Gradually the show began to ring true. Mary would have dates, but not "boyfriends." As co-producer Allan Burns says, "We never showed her in bed, but we were making it clear this was a girl who was having a sex life." Sometimes she was alone on a Saturday night (along with the viewers). She was an associate producer on a TV show—but sometimes not in control at all. She had good friends—but sometimes they were dopes. The humor came from normal reactions to normal situations.

Her boss on the show was Ed Asner as Lou Grant. He too was a '70s character. In the first episode he said, "You know what you got, Mary? Spunk!" He paused. "I hate spunk!" And that signaled an end to the spunky sitcom heroine of the '60s, and the birth of a real woman of the '70s.

The pleasures of Mary's show were not confined to single women. Single men laughed—and learned. They eavesdropped on the "girl talk" between Mary and Rhoda (Valerie Harper) and saw the other side of the dating dilemma—as well as what women expected or didn't expect from a man.

Of Mary's goody-goody image, Valerie cracked, "She likes a great big glass of cold milk—to wash down her birth control pill."

Mary enjoyed lampooning her own image. She and the MTM crew put together a private tape of bloopers and out-takes from the show and the highlight (repeated over and over) was Mary blowing a line and shouting out an unladylike four-letter word.

Onscreen Mary was the epitome of the liberated, dating single woman (with a becoming comic vulnerability). Offscreen she was outspoken. Her views on birth control, marijuana, gun control, and abortion didn't please the conservatives (or that crabby-looking woman who stared at her during the opening credits as she threw her hat into the air). She believed some elements of the "me generation" were healthier than a life of neurotic inhibition. "I'm only going to be here for a very short time," she'd tell interviewers, "and I have a right and an obligation to enjoy my life."

She enjoyed huge success. By the time she called it quits in the spring of 1977, Mary had racked up six Emmy awards, just two shy of all-time leader Dinah Shore. She became TV "royalty." When she did her infrequent talk show or print interview, she was usually treated with the awe accorded a Jackie Onassis and the respect paid a Lucille Ball.

Mary was also a successful business-

♥ **Mary and the gang, including David Letterman—one of her brave series' failures.**

woman. MTM Enterprises produced *The Bob Newhart Show, Hill Street Blues,* and many more. Obviously it was husband Grant Tinker who made MTM Enterprises a success, but after her show went off the air and Mary had more time, she developed an interest in the business world.

With her own company, Mary was in a unique position to produce her own projects. In 1978 she starred in a TV movie, *First You Cry.* A drama about a newswoman's breast cancer surgery, it won impressive reviews from critics who had doubted her serious acting ability.

Sadly, the tears that year were for real. Her young sister died of a drug overdose.

If the end of the '60s had been rough for Mary, the last years of the '70s were worse. In 1978 her hour-long variety show *Mary* lasted exactly three hours. After three weeks CBS pulled it off the air. As Mary recalled on David Letterman's talk show in 1987, "It was horrendous doing an hour-long show with music and choreography in five days. It was terrifying." Letterman had been a cast member on the show.

CBS tried *The Mary Tyler Moore Hour* in 1979, this time trying to blend sitcom and variety. She played Mary McKinnon, who, as the star of her own variety show,

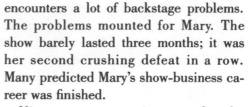

♥ Glittering: nominated for an Oscar, awarded a Tony, and showing off yet another Emmy.

encounters a lot of backstage problems. The problems mounted for Mary. The show barely lasted three months; it was her second crushing defeat in a row. Many predicted Mary's show-business career was finished.

Nineteen seventy-nine was also the year that Mary and Grant's marriage ended. Both soberly reported that after more than a decade, the marriage had simply run out of steam.

Nineteen eighty started with the worst trauma of all. Mary's son Richard killed himself.

Richard had been living with his father, Richard Meeker. Like his father, he'd developed a fanatical interest in guns and owned many. One night, after a phone call from his girlfriend that was reportedly ordinary and cheerful, he began idly loading and unloading a shotgun. While his roommate watched, he said, "She loves me," and pulled the trigger. It clicked emptily. He said "She loves me not." It clicked again. He said "She loves me."

There was no click; only the roar of a bullet crashing into his skull. He was dead a half hour later.

Mary's old friends rallied around her. Dick Van Dyke called her constantly, and Ed Asner literally gave her his shoulder to cry on during the long, painful nights.

Things could only get better after the past devastating years. For Mary, a sweetheart of the '60s and then a young working woman of the '70s, there was finally the promise of a natural progression into a mature woman of the '80s.

Spurned by TV, Mary turned to the stage and film work, making a dramatic comeback. She was nominated for an Oscar as the star of the drama *Ordinary People*, and received a special Tony for her role as a quadriplegic in *Who's Life is It Anyway?* The show, originally written for a male lead, was rewritten for her. At the time, this was new—and almost sacrilege. Now playwrights often adapt their plays for a change in gender (as Neil Simon did reviving *The Odd Couple*). Starting the '80s, Mary was forging new ground. Some stodgy critics complained. John Simon refused to believe that a quadriplegic woman would want to kill herself because her sex life was ruined. After all, that was only something a man would do. Perhaps he felt a woman's duty in bed was just to lie there and accommodate the man.

"Can you believe that Simon couldn't understand why Claire Harrison would want to die because her sex life was over?" Mary fumed. "God almighty! How dare anybody deny a woman's sexuality, how dare anybody imply that women are only the passive recipients of sex? Women enjoy sex, are aggressors at times—why in heaven's name not?"

Mary had to be aggressive to land Dr. Robert Levine, the nice-looking young doctor who was treating Mary's mother for bronchitis. When he told her to give him a call in case of emergency, she asked, "Does acute loneliness count?"

Attracted to him, she did what Mary Richards would have done—she stilled her inhibitions and called him up. Some

were surprised that Mary was attracted to this quiet young doctor, fifteen years younger than she. He wasn't the fatherly "authority" figure her other husbands had been. Her dates over the past few years had included a British millionaire (Sir Gordon White) and comedian Steve Martin.

"My love for Robert evolved quickly," she says. "It started as a strong attraction to a wonderful guy, and before I knew it I was a little in love, and then I was a lot in love, and then I was married!"

They were married on November 23, 1983, in New York, where Mary had set up her "bachelor apartment" after her TV shows failed. Said Valerie Harper, "Rhoda would have been so jealous— Mary got herself a Jewish doctor." On doctor's orders, Mary gave up a few bad habits—her lifelong smoking, and her "controlled alcoholism." She was never drunk but often needed a drink, which wasn't good for anyone, much less a diabetic.

A few years later, Mary decided to try television again. With her 1986 sitcom, she evidently was hoping to duplicate the success of the WJM newsroom on her old show, and Ed Asner's success with *Lou Grant*. The new setting was a newspaper office. The show bombed, a sign that an '80s woman cannot, or should not, go backward to the same format or style of a '70s woman.

Mary came into 1988 with a TV movie success, playing Mary Todd Lincoln. As usual, she had some fear about taking on such a demanding role, but as usual, she fought it. And then, she decided to try the sitcom world one more time.

"You need challenges, fears, uncertainty, a certain amount of crying at night . . . I still have that insecurity that they'll 'find me out,' that I don't deserve all this success. But I know that many people have that same feeling."

Mary isn't obsessed with proving she's a great dramatic actress, or necessarily becoming number 1 in sitcoms again. "I'm learning that it's okay . . . to let my hair down . . . (to do) the things I want to do, not what I should do . . . I've broken out of a shell. I'm looking at myself, rather than just smiling through life, denying emotions I've been afraid of. I did not want to go on being closed to myself, pretending, acting things out, having acquaintances instead of friends . . . I'm finding out who I am."

So far, what she's found out has pleased her. "I'm married to a wonderful man. I'm relatively healthy. I have enough money to keep me supplied and to contribute to other people's well-being. I'm pretty well off in every sense."

Eva Gabor ❀

GREEN ACRES

First broadcast: September 15, 1965
Last broadcast: September 7, 1971

She was the jet-set sophisticate. Her frosty meringue of coiffed platinum-blond hair and her playful Hungarian accent hinted of exotic European nobility and an elegant sense of hedonism. But when Eva Gabor's jet touched down amid the cows, pigs, and rurals of Hooterville, U.S.A., it really heightened her appeal: now she was accessible, the dream was down to earth.

Though she was a sexy starlet in the '40s and a popular Broadway actress in the '50s, it was as a '60s sweetheart that Eva achieved true stardom at last.

Just think: any kid on his paper route through Pixley to Hooterville (or "Hootersville" as she pronounced it) might spy Eva as glamorous ex–New Yorker Lisa Douglas. There she'd be, standing outside her improbable farm shack in one of her chiffon nightgown/dresses, her impish, tilted eyes and tart, good-natured grin seeming to say, "Naughty boy, vat in the world are you staring at?"

Green Acres was a "double spinoff." First came *The Beverly Hillbillies* and *Petticoat Junction*. *Green Acres* was set in the same sleepy American county as the latter, but was a variation on the former. Instead of Jed Clampett and his hillbillies moving from the big city to the country, here was Oliver Wendell Douglas, New York lawyer, bringing his wife out to live on a farm in the middle of nowhere.

Paul Henning produced all three shows, and one of his trademarks was a tell-all theme song explaining the premise. Oliver and Lisa duet on the joys of country life vs. city life: "The chores!" "The stores!" "Fresh air!" "Times Square!" Ultimately: "You are my wife!" "Good-bye, city life." And in vague harmony, "Green Acres, we are there."

The show was inspired by the dimly remembered radio show, *Granby's Green Acres*, which ironically starred Bea Benaderet, later of *Petticoat Junction*. The casting was set right from the start. Eddie Albert, a real-life gardening and fitness buff, would play Oliver. And Lisa would be played by . . . Martha Hyer. When Hyer dropped out of the negotiations, twenty-six other actresses tried out for the role. Execs weren't even considering Eva. They complained about her "funny" accent. But Eva vowed to take the part, and even did her own makeup and hair for the screen test. She succeeded, of course, and made it look easy. That's the mark of a professional, and all through her career, she's been just that: a disciplined, determined actress, the opposite of her frothy image.

Eva, the youngest of the three Gabor sisters, was born in Budapest on February 11. She gives the year as 1926 but most writers have given it back. Sources generally say 1921.

Her father was a jeweler, prosperous enough to send his daughters to fine schools and provide a governess to teach them grace and charm. Eva was always interested in acting, though her father wasn't enthusiastic about the lowly profession.

In 1939, the aspiring young actress met Dr. Eric Drimmer, an osteopath from Hollywood who had come to Hungary on a three-day visit. She met him at a party, and the impressionable girl could hardly control herself. She was barely five foot one, and he was six foot four. She thought he was "a Norse god," and she let her mind race into fantasy: if he proposed to her, she would accept!

That night he *did* propose. But then he had to go back to America. For three months the two wrote intense letters to each other. Looking back on it all, Eva sees the humor in this lovesick situation. Mooning over her Norse god, she recalled that his face was everywhere: "If I opened a can of sardines, there he lay, all six feet four, in olive oil."

Finally the couple arranged a compromise. They met in London and got married there. Then it was back to Hollywood and the glamorous life of a budding actress. Only, as Eva quickly found out, it wasn't very glamorous and there was no shortage of starlets trying to bud into showbiz.

Eva knew very little English, the doctor was just starting his practice, and the couple lived modestly. The Hungarian housewife was alone much of the day, with no friends and a world of strangers speaking a language she could only vaguely understand. Worst of all, Hollywood had a different idea of beauty than she did. To them, her looks were from Hungary. They didn't need a woman with mouse-brown hair and a well-fed figure.

♥ **1940s publicity shots stressed Eva's exotic and playful nature.**

Eva toned up her middle, studied hard to learn English, and graduated to the level of starlet at Paramount. She was exotic, her accent intriguing, but not necessarily for feature parts. In 1941 she made a film called *Forced Landing*. As Eva says, "It was a B picture only to those too lazy to go down the alphabet."

She and her Norse god were divorced in 1942. Through the '40s Eva continued to toil away as decoration in a variety of forgotten films *(A Royal Scandal,* 1945; *Wife of Monte Cristo,* 1946; *Song of Surrender,* 1949). Meanwhile the rest of the family had arrived, and the gossip columns were no longer boring but Gaboring. Sari, now called Zsa Zsa, was a favorite. Her loves and lovers made consistent headlines. And then there was third sister Magda, helping to confuse matters.

Eva was the one who wanted to be taken seriously as an actress, but it was difficult to keep the Gabor sisters straight, and tough for a '40s starlet to balance valuable, sexy publicity with a desire to play deeper, romantic roles in major movies. It was a frustrating time for her.

She came to Broadway in 1950 for *The Happy Time,* and began to carve out a stage career balancing light roles with ones of more substance. She played opposite Noël Coward in *Present Laughter,* and replaced Vivien Leigh in *Tovarich.* She was in everything from *Blithe Spirit* and *A Shot in the Dark* to *Oh Men, Oh Women.* She was part of the "Golden Age" of television, too, starring in a production of *Uncle Vanya* with Boris Karloff.

Her private life was less successful. In her 1954 autobiography, *Orchids and Salami,* she wrote, "I have been both hunter and hunted, and what depresses me is that in either role I'm usually the one who gets hurt." She, like the other Gabors, went through multiple marriages that failed "due to the old conflict between home and career . . . not because I am the Playgirl of the Western World."

At least she was wise and worldly when it came to seeing through the "sex goddess" syndrome. She was gracious toward autograph seekers and panting admirers, but at the same time sidestepped their advances and maintained her dignity. Today she sums up the male predatory instinct this way: "The man's point of view, and I don't agree with it, is having sex just for the reason of having sex. Now women should never do that. A woman would become cheap then. And in my mind there's nothing worse than a used woman. We have to keep ourselves on a rather high level, I think. I always have."

Sometimes there were hefty temptations. A ninety-three-year-old man sent Eva a polite letter informing her that he probably hadn't too much longer to live, had $370,000 in the bank, and required only "a modicum of companionship" from her if she would become his wife. In her autobiography she wrote, "It is disturbing to receive proposals in the mail from men who are lonely and whose concepts of love and marriage as something you can find in a Sears Roebuck catalogue inspire them to write these mildly insane notes in full expectation of being taken seriously."

Eva's marriages were to non-show-business types: a realtor, a surgeon, a stockbroker, and an aeronautics executive. Her most exotic affair was with Tyrone Power, but she kept it discreet. Even so, she had the reputation of being a sex star living a rich, exotic lifestyle. Zsa Zsa, married to George Sanders, had an affair with playboy Porfiro Rubirosa. When Sanders and a photographer came crashing through a window on the naked couple, it was a sensational scandal. Since it happened "to one of the Gabor sisters," the publicity rubbed off on Eva, too. Some thought Eva was the one married to Sanders. Some thought it was Zsa Zsa who had all the big Broadway credits.

Igor Cassini seemed to sum up Eva and her sisters in the public's mind. He lumped them all together as "the ultimate playgirls. With over sixteen husbands—or is it more—between them, to marry into the family you don't have to be crazy but it helps." In fact, George Sanders may have proved his insanity by marrying Magda some time after his divorce from Zsa Zsa.

Eva continued to balance the role of "sex star" and the profession of actress, trying to emphasize the wit and intelligence behind the allure. Still, many attributed Zsa Zsa's one-liners to her, or made comparisons between the two. The only thing Eva hated more than that was when someone would compliment her—by criticizing Zsa Zsa.

She doesn't mind most of the jokes about the two of them and their love lives. When Zsa Zsa married again recently, a TV interviewer asked:

"Did you go to your sister's wedding?"

"No."

"Why not?"

"Well, you can't make them all!"

The confusion between Zsa Zsa and Eva has always been a sore spot, but sometimes Eva can make it worse. Last year she met Ann Landers. She asked, "Which vun are you, dahling, are you

Ann or are you your sister, Abigail Van Buren?" Ann replied, "Which one are you, dahling, are you Eva or Zsa Zsa?"

There was less confusion after Eva followed the 1964 film *Youngblood Hawke* with the hit TV show *Green Acres*, about a mythical farm located somewhere outside Chicago: "You just have to change planes twice, then you take a bus from the county seat to Pixley and take a little train to Hooterville."

The role model of a sexy, loving wife, Eva was warm, patient and remarkably good-natured. In the pilot, when Oliver makes wild plans to move to the farm, she stares in surprise, but quickly compromises. She accepts his eccentricity and asks for a six-month trial period to see if they can live the farm life. She's almost an indulgent mother to her boyishly irrepressible Oliver. Perhaps right there adolescent boys fell in love with her: the motherly "older" woman of forty who is also an erotic wife evidently well armed with a Frederick's of Hollywood mail-order catalog.

Eva was the least threatening, yet most authentic version of the European "woman of the world" that TV had yet seen. Within the limits of '60s TV, Eva was worldly and intriguing, but never scary. Pairing her with bland ol' Eddie Albert, the show seemed to be saying that any guy, no matter how much the stodgy straight arrow, had a chance to grow up and court royalty!

She was no brassy Alice deflating a bubble-headed Ralph Kramden. She loved Oliver, mothered him, and com-

forted him. When Oliver, in the pilot, tells her he is going to take her away from luxurious New York and dump her in the middle of nowhere, she doesn't scowl at the scheme. "My roots are in the soil," Oliver exults. "So that's what you want to do," Lisa says with a sexy, sulky pout of disapproval, "soil your roots!" Wide-eyed Oliver babbles, "I take a little seed, I put it in the ground, I put dirt over it, I water it, and then do you know what I get?" Lisa nods. "A dirty little wet seed."

Through 170 episodes she put up with

Oliver, with inept carpenters Alf and Ralph (Sid Melton and Mary Canfield), scheming Mr. Haney (Pat Buttram), and the rest of the cast. Eva was funny on *Green Acres,* but not in the mode of a Lucille Ball. She was often put in incongruous, slapstick-type situations but never lost dignity. The humor was gentle, coming more from her confusion over farm life and custom. Like *The Beverly Hillbillies,* the show had no malice in its satirical comparisons of city and country life. And, like that show, it was an instant hit. It was in the Top 10 in 1967, and in the Top 20 the next two years.

Women made up a good portion of the audience. Eva showed the women of Middle America how to be glamorous even in the most mundane surroundings. They admired the gowns she wore and the graceful ease she showed, even when confronted by the wayward resident of the neighboring Ziffel farm, Arnold the Pig. Eva didn't win any Emmys, but Arnold the Pig won two Patsy Awards.

The show's running gags generally featured Eva the Innocent humorously confronted by rustic miseries, from shaky farm machinery and tractors to rusty pumps and weak flooring. Here was a woman of charming naïveté, delicately huffing in mild exasperation over her chores, who obviously needed her man around the house. *But,* she was also, at other times, the self-assured and seductive wife. And, of course, every now and then there was a bit of sexy innuendo to keep viewers alert. After a day of chores Lisa confides to Kate Bradley (Bea

Benaderet), "I've had it, in places I've never had it before."

Today some might object to Lisa Douglas as too much the stereotype of the wife subservient to her husband. But back in the '60s Eva Gabor was the warm, vivacious wife any growing boy would have loved to call his own, and on viewing today, she still exudes that basic affection missing from so many sitcoms of the '80s, shows that are too often all wisecrack and insult. And she displays, in her costumes and demeanor, pride and confidence in herself as a woman. She dresses not for her husband but for herself.

Eva worked hard on the show. She would be up at 4:30 every morning, and often worked until 8:30 at night. Even during these sixteen-hour days, cast members were amazed at Gabor's grace and even temper. She was a "team player," working along with Eddie Albert and the rest of the cast to make the show a success. In fact, if anyone was prone to joking, it was Albert. Always in trim shape, Eddie once slipped out of his robe, and standing in just his boxer shorts, grinned and said, "Eat your heart out, Eva!"

In 1983 Eddie and Eva reteamed for the Broadway show *You Can't Take It with You.* "Eddie and I were leaving the theater," she recalls, "and found ourselves surrounded by a large group of kids. Suddenly, they broke into a chorus of the *Green Acres* theme song. It was very funny and very sweet."

Green Acres peaked in popularity in 1967. The hippies were arriving and the Woodstock generation didn't adopt the Eva Gabor image of back-to-the-farm elegance. Poor Eva complained to columnist Kay Gardella in 1968, "Can you imagine being married to one of those men? Why you'd get fleas! In fact you can't find flea collars anyplace today, the hippies buy them all." She was repulsed by the bearded guys in dirty jeans and had no kind words for their companions: "I hate what women are doing to themselves today . . . I don't remember the last time I saw a feminine woman dressed properly with hat, gloves and perfume on."

The show barely staggered into 1970. Eva's still proud of the show, but prouder of what she accomplished in 1970, when the green went out of Green Acres. She formed her own Gabor International, and it's grown into the world's largest wig company, with sales figures that are so far into the millions that "It's frightening, darling." Acting is "the most wonderful profession in the world, but you can't work all the time. But you have to eat all the time." She relishes her job as chairman of the board of Gabor International, and is far from being a mere figurehead for the wig company.

Her personal life has become more solid, too. True, her last two marriages ended in divorce, but each lasted about a decade. When her latest ended in 1983, she found it wasn't quite so difficult to live alone. She enjoys her newfound independence. "I've grown up," she says. "You must learn to look out for yourself." In an interview with Dr. Ruth Westheimer she explained, "All my life I was a clinging wife . . . it's the stupid European upbringing that man is almighty . . ."

Just as she worked a balance between city and country life on *Green Acres*, Eva can see the balance necessary in a relationship. She believes the feminists are "doing it all wrong. Because the women who go out and say 'I am as good as a man'—they are like men. I am a female female. I always have been. I adore men." But it's also important "to be strong . . . we have to be very bright and watch ourselves because we are born alone and we die alone."

Generally on the talk-show circuit Eva keeps to her image, offering double entendres that embarrass rather than shock. Just her presence was enough to fluster David Letterman. The tongue-tied host looked down at his desk and muttered, "I'm having a bad day." Eva shook her head, and grinned: "You're having a good day, I've never seen you more up."

Although there is the "Gabor image" of sauciness and cheerful decadence, there's quite a difference between the fantasy and real life. She believes in some old-fashioned virtues, like marriage. In 1980, when she conducted a television tour of her home (a five-million-dollar house once owned by Frank Sinatra and Mia Farrow), she pointed to the bedroom, "Where no man ever came but a husband." Today she adds, "The only reason to have sex is because you love somebody. Just to do it is a lot of exercise for no reason at all. It's a waste of energy and time."

Eva has a full schedule these days. She takes on acting parts (she was on *Edge of Night* and enjoys summer stock productions), she lectures on "Living Alone and Loving It," and promotes Gabor wigs: "I make appearances in department stores. You can't believe how strong women can be. I have ten cops around me. Still they pull your hair off if they can. It scares the hell out of me . . . women are dear and sweet and lovely, darling, but they can make a crepe suzette out of you."

In 1985 her mother, Jolie, who owns a jewelry store in New York, underwent cosmetic surgery. "My mother was the most beautiful woman in Hungary. And if you get to mother's age, but not before—because I can't stand those pulled-up faces—and you want to look beautiful, why not . . . but I believe you should wait till the very last moment. I haven't done it yet if that's what you're wondering. I'm very lucky. I have good bone structure."

On the cable TV show *Alive and Well*, Eva was asked how she stayed beautiful. "Beauty comes from within," she said. "Beauty is not outside, because you can get bored even looking at a Renoir painting, which is my favorite painter in the world. You look at it, you look at it, and then you say, well, it's a piece of art, but that's not enough in life. You have to have rare beauty and that comes from the soul, so I hope I have a lovely soul."

The American Rose Society thinks she has a beautiful body and soul. They named a rose after her. Don't expect Eva to act like a flower and stay out in the sun: "I never, ever go in the sun. I play tennis with a hat, swim with a hat . . ."

Careful about her health and diet, she doesn't smoke, rarely eats meat and stays away from alcohol. "I don't drink any hard liquor, although I like a little wine and champagne . . . as far as the dope that people take, I mean, life is difficult to face if you have all your faculties. But if you are dumb from dope—I don't know how they do it."

For several years, the love of her life has been Merv Griffin. In the winter of 1988, Merv gave her a $100,000 diamond-and-pearl necklace with a 20-carat topaz centerpiece. Sometimes their ro-mance has been a lot lighter than that. They were seen playing doubles at a celebrity tennis match. When they jumped into the lead on the first point, and the announcer cried out "Fifteen-love," Eva gave Merv a kiss. He admonished her, "They said 'love' not 'sex'!"

She remains forever young, forever a symbol of elegance and good living. It's just that today her definition of good living and good sex has matured.

"The best part of lovemaking," she says, "is afterward. When you talk and laugh."

♥ A familiar pose—Eva gets married in a 1983 guest spot on *Hart to Hart*.

Elizabeth Montgomery ✿

BEWITCHED

First broadcast: September 17, 1964
Last broadcast: July 1, 1972

"I'm not trying to put *Bewitched* down," says Elizabeth Montgomery. "I've just reached another plateau in the type of work I want to do. It's like a man working all his life as a gardener and suddenly waking up to the fact that he wants to be a landscape architect. I want to act—believe me—because that's what I do best."

Actually, her role as Samantha Stevens did require good acting, especially since the sitcom plots on *Bewitched* were too bewildering to bother with. Jack O'Brian, in the *New York Journal-American*, saw it right from the start:

"Miss Montgomery is a uniquely equipped amulet for this feathery hocus-pocus. She has beauty, youth and a splendid subtlety in her reactions, able to register many a mood most girls would indicate simply by sticking out their tongues; she manages with the merest moves, eyelash batting and eyefuls of dancing glints, in her admirably suppressed 'takes' and just-barely grimaces and amused gloatings."

Acting, in any form, was what Elizabeth wanted, early on, even though she admits that her father, actor Robert Montgomery, was not encouraging. "Dad never taught me the tricks of the trade. When I was a child he painted as black a picture as possible of the acting business."

Born in Los Angeles on April 15, 1933, Elizabeth spent eleven years under the scrupulous care of the Westlake School for Girls. When her father moved to New York to do his own TV show, the family moved too. Elizabeth completed her education at the Spence School. From there she spent two years at the American Academy of Dramatic Arts. She made her TV debut on December 3, 1951, on *Robert Montgomery Presents*. The name of the episode was "Top Secret"—the secret being that Mr. Montgomery didn't know his daughter had tried out for—and won—the role until rehearsals began. She made her stage debut on October 13, 1953, in *Late Love* with Arlene Francis.

The fluffy play did not get good reviews. Ingenue Elizabeth was noticed mostly for her heritage, not acting. Critics referred to her as "Robert Montgomery's daughter." Walter Kerr wrote: "Robert Montgomery's daughter Elizabeth is trim, pretty and attractively petulant as a lovelorn youngster." Another critic, John Chapman, after mentioning Robert Montgomery, did notice the daughter had some traits the elder didn't: "one perky nose and two perky buzzooms."

In March 1954 she married socially prominent Fred Cammann. In August 1955 she divorced him. That year she made her first important film, *The Court Martial of Billy Mitchell*. In 1956 she was the female lead in the short-lived Broadway comedy *The Loud Red Patrick*.

Each year in New York had been a new adventure. When Elizabeth moved back to Hollywood, things mellowed. She married Gig Young, and the partnership lasted six years. During that time, she made two hundred TV appearances. For "The Rusty Heller Story," an episode of *The Untouchables*, she received an Emmy nomination. But the winner, nominated in the same category, was Judith Anderson in *Macbeth*.

Elizabeth played comedies and dramas, eager to learn. She didn't care what TV critics said—the important criticism came from her father. "Dad is brutally frank when he criticizes my performances," she told writer Vernon Scott. "He never gives me a pat on the head when I deserve a rap on the knuckles." Once, after a slightly histrionic dramatic role, Robert firmly told her, "If I ever catch you acting like Theda Bara again I'll kill you!"

In 1963, the year before *Betwitched*, movie audiences saw Dean Martin be tender with her in *Who's Been Sleeping in My Bed* and Henry Silva be tough with her as *Johnny Cool*. Paramount had been grooming her as a very sultry, super-bewitching sex symbol, five foot eight in heels.

When she met *Johnny Cool* director William Asher, she recalled, "We loathed each other on first sight." Soon they were both bewitched. Asher divorced his wife. Elizabeth and Gig Young split, and then Asher and Montgomery married in Mexico in October of 1963.

Though *Johnny Cool* had guest appearances by everyone from Mort Sahl to Telly Savalas, Sammy Davis, Jr., to Joey Bishop, critics only liked Liz. *The New York Times* deplored "the flaccid direction

sitcoms like *My Living Doll*, *The Addams Family*, and *The Munsters*.

Mr. and Mrs. Asher filmed their pilot episode of *Bewitched* in November of 1963. They drew some elements from the Kim Novak movie *Bell, Book and Candle*, but seemed to pay closer attention to *My Favorite Martian* (where "superhuman" lives with "human" while the neighbors are comically suspicious) and to *The Dick Van Dyke Show*.

Like Dick Van Dyke, Dick York was a lean and gawky suburbanite with a nice job, comfy house, and pretty housewife. Like Mary Tyler Moore, Elizabeth

♥ **Starlet days: Elizabeth plays it soft and sultry in some Paramount publicity poses.**

of William Asher," but not the scenes that featured Elizabeth Montgomery, especially "when she does her soul-searching wearing nothing more than a becoming lap robe . . . Miss Montgomery, without benefit of wardrobe, attracts more attention than the entire uncomfortable [cast]."

After *Johnny Cool* the loving Ashers decided that they formed a great team, on-camera as well as off, and wanted to produce a TV show together. The big trend in 1962–63 was fantasy. Horror movies and magazines were a fad, and *My Favorite Martian* a successful new show. The coming year would offer supernatural

Montgomery was sexy but safe. Samantha Stevens was a housewife who acted more like a housecat: comfortable, but occasionally stricken with naughty, impish impulses. Like Moore's Laura Petrie, she could be independent when she chose to be.

Off-camera, Elizabeth was very much the housewife; an attractive, lively complement to her stocky, cigarillo-chomping, Lou Grant-ish hubby. Not surprisingly, Asher had a less than feminist point of view on *Bewitched*. He said at the time, "The show portrays a mixed marriage that overcomes by love the enormous obstacles in its path. Samantha, in her new role as housewife, represents the true values in life. Material gains mean nothing to her. She can have anything she wants through witchcraft yet she'd rather scrub the kitchen floor on her hands and knees for the man she loves. It is emotional satisfaction she craves."

When *Bewitched* was sold, Elizabeth was pregnant. The first five episodes were shot around her, but in order to keep to her director-husband's schedule, she had to bounce back just three weeks after childbirth to hit the 5:30 A.M.-to-7:30 P.M. grind of sitcom work. It was a challenge, and she accepted it willingly, but those first months were hell.

Eventually Elizabeth's home resounded with the patter of tiny feet. It was her son chasing the family pet, a Siamese cat named Zip-Zip.

As *Bewitched* developed, the patient, loving, always attractive Samantha would somehow get into the middle of unpredictable situations where she would have to use her witchcraft—which was really just an exaggerated form of "feminine wiles." Under the surface of this very mild sitcom was a strong, intriguing undercurrent: the idea that no matter how secure and successful a man could be, he had almost no control over his woman. She proved what husbands suspected all the time—live with your wife long enough, and she reveals herself to be a witch! The cartoon that opened the show said it all: pop-eyed, confused, sweaty Dick York is totally flustered as his beautiful wife turns herself from

♥ **A flick of the wrist and a raised eyebrow—some of the subtle witchery of Samantha Stevens.**

a cuddly sex kitten groveling at his feet into a beautiful wife who jumps into his arms expecting his support—and keeping his hands full forevermore. If the ordinary woman can lead a man around the block by a swivel of her hips, here was a witch who could create complete chaos with a twitch of her cute little nose! It was this conflict that kept *Bewitched* fresh for at least the first half of its 254 episodes.

In episode after episode, Darin was constantly bedeviled by his witchy wife. Fortunately for him, she didn't have a vindictive temper—her anger was more a collection of cute grimaces, pert pouts, big-sisterly groans, and an occasionally lip-biting look of perplexity. The war between mortal man and super-witch was evenly matched because, for reasons unknown, Samantha loved him. Perhaps, in director William Asher's scenario, it was because she craved the stability of being the total housewife to him. Anyway, it was that love that made Darin more than a wimp—for no matter how helpless he was, Darin never lost his ire and his anger. He knew that if he walked out on Samantha, she couldn't take it. And so he would stand up to the endless witch friends of Samantha—including mother-in-law Endora (played by Agnes Moorehead), even if she called him "Durwood" and regularly made a monkey out of him by turning him into a bird, beast, or inanimate object.

When it premiered, *Bewitched* got the best reviews of any 1964 sitcom. It was "a most beguiling and devilishly funny comedy," according to the *Denver Post. Time*

magazine called it "the surprising runaway champion of all the new TV shows," and marveled at the way Elizabeth could twitch her nose "in a unique and peculiar manner that seems to be half allergy and half tic douloureau [sic]."

The show was good enough to go without explanatory lyrics in the theme song—something most '60s shows seemed to find essential. Maybe the reason was that the lyrics were so incredibly bad nobody would want to sing them: "You witch, you witch, one thing is for sure. That stuff you pitch just hasn't got a cure . . ."

The pilot episode did offer a flashback, explaining how Samantha and Darin met—by accident. They just kept bumping into each other, in stores and on the street. It was destiny, not witchcraft. Of course, some wedding nights are better than others—on theirs, she told him she was a witch!

The silly sitcom's success was due to its stars—the underrated Dick York as straight man, and the remarkable Elizabeth Montgomery as Samantha. Elizabeth, like Mary Tyler Moore, was not a comedienne. She had a few cutely funny traits (like her appealingly timid "Well . . ." after Darin discovered her latest naughtiness and demanded an explanation), but basically the fascination was in her dual nature—the sweet-tempered housewife, and the eyebrow-raising, nose-twitching, slightly evilly grinning, in-control witch.

Bewitched was the number 2 show when it really hit its stride in 1965. Like *The Dick Van Dyke Show*, which was also going strong in 1965, *Bewitched* benefited from a strong ensemble. Van Dyke's show had experienced character comics like Rose Marie and Morey Amsterdam; Montgomery could play off next-door neighbors George Tobias (Abner) and Alice Pearce (Gladys). Van Dyke had a bland flunky (Richard Deacon as Mel) and a boss hanging over his head (Carl Reiner as Alan Brady); Dick York had it worse: the bland but always pesty and nervous David White as boss Larry Tate, and Agnes Moorehead as the deliciously wicked mother-in-law Endora, who was always ready with an endearing remark like "You have the retentive powers of a dodo bird."

There was also Aunt Clara (Marion Lorne), Dr. Bombay (Bernard Fox), Uncle Arthur (Paul Lynde), and eventually Sam's father (Maurice Evans), all fine actors able to contribute colorful support.

On the set, Elizabeth was generally even-tempered, and Asher firm. They showed some affection, but the atmosphere was very professional. Once Elizabeth stopped during the rehearsal of a scene, trying to recall the next lines of dialogue. "Where are we?" she called out.

"Stage 4. *Bewitched*," Asher answered dryly. "Shall we continue?"

With fourteen-hour days, Liz and Bill valued their privacy and the time they could spend with their young children. They liked bike riding for exercise, and one of Elizabeth's favorite forms of creative relaxation was painting and drawing. She admired Andrew Wyeth's work, and had a very homey touch of her own. Magazines sometimes printed a few of her whimsical drawings, including cute, crookedly smiling self-portraits of the innocently witchy Samantha.

Bewitched was in the Top 10 through 1967, lasting longer than *The Munsters*, *The Addams Family*, and most other gimmick-fantasy shows. It lost some magic at the turn of the '70s. The show used sitcom tricks that were already old hat, including the old "lookalike" wheeze, with Montgomery playing Serena, Samantha's evil cousin, and the old "baby" wheeze— trying to make the aging show feel new with the birth of Tabitha, a witch daughter. When Tabitha got dull, another baby arrived, Adam, a warlock son. It was no occasion for passing out cigars; just for passing out. The earlier supporting players either died or left the show, replaced by an irritating collection of next-door neighbors and childish witches and warlocks who seemed to exist for no reason except to perpetrate dopey practical jokes on Sam and Darin.

Through it all, Samantha remained cool, calm, with all the forgiveness of a kindergarten teacher. In one episode, she and Darin journey back to Salem, Massachusetts. She asserted that none of the women put on trial and later burned were witches. She told the good folk of Salem, "The people you persecuted were guiltless, they were mortals just like yourselves. *You* are guilty." Even in the face of a holocaust, she never lost her tolerance. She might just as well have been lecturing Tabitha about hitting her teddy bear.

Though it might have been just a coincidence, the show dropped out of the Top 20 for good after the 1969–70 season when Dick York left the cast due to health problems. First he suffered back problems, then emphysema. In 1988, at sixty, he was confined to an oxygen machine: "Look at me, I have a hose up my nose and I haven't been out of the house for a year." Working for the Salvation Army from his home, York says, "The fact that I'm dying doesn't stop me from feeling very much alive, because death is a beautiful thing. It's the final answer to all pain . . . there's nothing to be scared of."

York was replaced by sitcom veteran Dick Sargent, whose real name was the doubly suggestive Dick Cox. Only four days younger than Elizabeth, he was a younger, milder Darin. Not that he didn't get mad or start whining when confronted by witches and warlocks. Not that, when told to "stop crowing," he didn't continue—and get turned into a crow.

Of course neither Dick was particularly well matched to one's fantasy of a husband for Elizabeth. They were both handsome in only a sitcom way, which let all the young men in the audience fantasize about being just funny-looking and/or good-looking enough to attract their own Samantha.

One memorable fantasy episode had Waldo the Warlock (Hal England) conjure up a fake Samantha who keeps telling him, "I love you." Waldo, very similar to any adolescent tuning in, loved having this doll-like fantasy girl spouting "I love you" at him even if it naturally made Darin and Larry Tate turn purple thinking it was the real Samantha. "It's a foolish fantasy," Waldo says, "but a harmless one." Caught by Samantha, he vowed to never indulge in such fantasizing again. But, in rerun, Samantha tempts new generations of young men, again and again.

Elizabeth never went in for much makeup, never tried to stylize her natural beauty. She never even bothered to fix her slightly chipped front tooth. "It's my snaggletooth," she said proudly. "All witches have one. I don't think it's worth going to a dentist and spending hundreds of dollars to repair it. You couldn't cap just that one, you'd have to do them all. And you'd end up with a mouth full of Chiclets."

As Samantha Stevens, Elizabeth was nominated for many Emmy awards, losing five times—once to Mary Tyler Moore, and twice each to Lucille Ball and Hope Lange. But she should've won something just for coming up with a different look of sweet contrition every time Darin popped his eyes and cried "You did *what?*"

The show ended and, eventually, so did Elizabeth's marriage to William Asher. "Divorce is not as big a bugaboo as it was years ago," she said, "and if it's handled openly and honestly, especially if there are children involved, which there were with Bill and me, I think it's fine."

Following the amicable divorce, Asher married Joyce Boulifant, a sitcom and quiz-show perennial noted for her blond, ditsy characterizations. Elizabeth did not marry—but chose a long-lasting live-in relationship with actor Robert Foxworth, whom she met doing a TV movie, *Mrs. Sundance*, in 1974.

After *Bewitched*, Elizabeth found TV movies the perfect vehicles for her dramatic needs. She started a bit slowly, with *The Victim* in 1972. It had a creaky "cat and the canary" plot (she's alone in a spooky house—a killer on the loose and her sister dead), but at least it wasn't a sitcom. From there, Elizabeth accepted only TV movies that tried to tackle important issues, or were professionally challenging. *A Case of Rape* was one of her important early TV movies. She was nominated for an Emmy, but lost to Cicely Tyson for *The Autobiography of Miss Jane Pittman.* Whenever she lost an Emmy for a TV movie, it was always to a star like that. She was nominated for *The Legend of Lizzie Borden,* but her competition that year was Katharine Hepburn, who won for her role in *Love Among the Ruins.* Nominated for *The Awakening Land,* Montgomery lost to Meryl Streep for *Holocaust.* Though she didn't always come away with the prize, the quality of Elizabeth Montgomery's work put her in the company of the leading actresses of the day.

Over the past decade, she has experimented with a variety of roles: She was a victim of a mugging in *Act of Violence,* and, on the flip side, Lizzie Borden, who, (in this TV movie) avoided blood-stained clothing by killing her parents in the nude. She played Belle Starr in a TV movie bio, a terminally ill woman *(Dark Victory),* a self-sufficient blind woman *(Second Sight).* She played a detective who falls in love with her black partner (O. J. Simpson in *A Killing Affair),* and was cast as a semi-hardboiled amateur detective in a noble experiment that proved to be ridiculous: *Missing Pieces.* In *Rules of Marriage* she had to deal with the pain and confusion of a "perfect" relationship gone wrong, and the effect of divorce on her children. In *Jennifer* she starred as a woman trying to hold onto her late husband's shipping firm while discovering the treachery of the business world.

In 1977, ABC tried to resurrect *Be-*

witched with a spin-off, *Tabitha*. But it wasn't Elizabeth Montgomery. So, *zap!*

In 1979 Elizabeth signed a deal with CBS that paid her $275,000 per film. The price would rise over the years. Add to that wise investments and the immense profits from *Bewitched* (of which she and Asher were part-owners) and the figure becomes impressive indeed.

Keeping her integrity and staying visible in important TV movie roles wasn't always easy. Sometimes even the most determined efforts to produce something substantial were in vain. Elizabeth recalls failing in her bid to bypass network censors in order to film a scene in *A Killing Affair* as the script intended—with O. J. Simpson and her together in bed. When the combination of black, white, and bed didn't make it to the screen, Montgomery voiced her displeasure, complaining to the press, "The networks really underestimate the public, their sophistication, their ability to cope with things that go on every day. And it annoys me that the censorship has gotten to a point where they will not face reality. It's stupid and childish."

Ironically, as Elizabeth Montgomery pursues each TV movie challenge—each "reality"—reruns of *Bewitched* continue to present beguiling fantasy. Sometimes stupid and childish, some episodes still bewitching and bedeviling, *Bewitched* still amuses audiences. Maybe inside every housewife, even the happy ones, there is that little bit of Samantha the witch. And inside every man there's a Darin fascinated by his wife's sorcery.

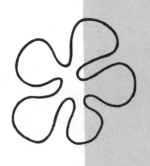

Comic Cuties

Judy Carne

THE BAILEYS OF BALBOA

First broadcast: September 24, 1964
Last broadcast: April 1, 1965

LOVE ON A ROOFTOP

First broadcast: September 13, 1966
Last broadcast: August 31, 1967

LAUGH-IN

First broadcast: January 22, 1968
Last broadcast: May 14, 1973

"Sock it to me, sock it to me, sock it to me!"

That said it all, didn't it?

On *Laugh-In*, Judy Carne strutted around in sexy outfits begging to be "socked." She usually got a pail of water thrown over her head, which temporarily cooled her off, but her message was clear: Sex is fun!

Everything about Judy said sex is fun: she had a peppy personality with pixie-short hair, a cute upturned nose, and sweet brown eyes. She had that adorable British accent, and she looked great in a bikini. So look *that* up in your Funk & Wagnall's. Definition of sex: fun!

Sex '60s style, carnality à la Carne, was supposed to be lighthearted and liberating. The promise of free love was right there on the screen. *Laugh-In* was the naïve side of the '60s revolution. The Vietnam War was lampooned with cornball jokes. The show's brightly flowered sets suggested the happy side of drug use.

And Judy Carne was right there offering a good time: "Sock it to me, sock it to me, sock it to me!"

Judy wasn't kidding—she lived that lifestyle. While Roger Miller sang that silly '60s tune "Eng-a-land swings like a pendulum do," Judy was swinging. Her free lifestyle in the '60s was a contrast to her strict younger years.

Judy was born in Northamptonshire, England, on April 27, 1939. Her name was Joyce Botterill then. Sent off to dance lessons at three, Joyce was a British Shirley Temple, adorable in her lacy little dresses, the center of attention at local talent shows. She was sent to the Bush-Davies school, where the headmistress eyed the girl's feet and foresaw a brilliant future for her. All it would take was the small feat of training.

The little ballerina learned that basic training for ballet was like basic training for war. She was subjected to intense discipline, even beatings. When her parents saw the bruises on their daughter's legs, they were alarmed, but reasoned that the teachers were just trying to cane some sense into the girl. After all, their Joyce was somewhat headstrong and independent.

The independence showed through. The fourteen-year-old girl found herself attracted to the headmistress's son—and she risked everything to sneak out at night to see him. She aggressively sought her first kiss—which startled the young lad. The clumsiness of their kissing was matched by the clumsiness of keeping things secret. Joyce was found out and duly punished—with her parents' sober approval.

Joyce would have to change. The head of the Bush-Davies school, Miss Bush herself, even changed the sixteen-year-old's name. Miss Bush called her Judy. Judy then adopted the last name of a character she'd played in a school play, Sarah Carne.

The disciplined, newly named Judy Carne danced her way to London's West End, appearing in musical comedy revues. The West End actor's world was wild—and Judy didn't need any coaxing to shake off the shackles and learn to live it up. She made up her mind to lose her virginity to a cast member in a play she was in. As she described it in her autobiography, "I expected fireworks, trumpets, and earthquakes. What I got was a quick roll in a field, with few words spoken and many tears shed. I thought perhaps I had done something wrong, and was miserably disappointed."

That she had to play opposite the guy throughout the play's run was also a miserable experience, but Judy got over it. Besides, there were plenty of other actors around. Judy won a part on an episode of Patrick MacGoohan's *Secret Agent* show and was infatuated. But he was married, and told her so gently but emphatically.

Judy met others. Race car driver Sterling Moss amazed her with his James Bond-style apartment, complete with push-button gimmicks in the bedroom and luxurious bathtubs. Vidal Sassoon gave her a short haircut and, in a scene out of *Some Like It Hot*, the diffident and

Latin lover by the name of Desi Arnaz. On the loose from Lucy, Desi invited Judy to a ranch he owned and brought her to the stables. Snuggling close to her, Desi tried the ultimate in visual aphrodisiacs: he had her watch two horses having sex. Right before Judy's eyes a mare was tied down and made ready for the sport. A stud stallion was brought in, and Judy was duly impressed, the horse's "phallus growing so immense it almost dragged in the dirt." Stable-owner Arnaz grew feverish as he watched the spectacle, pointing out every detail to Judy, excitedly describing what was going to happen next.

♥ Serious young starlet: Judy Carne starts her career. Photo courtesy of *Movie Star News.*

♥ In costume for her hit show *The Boyfriend.*

apathetic man was seduced by eager Judy. She didn't use the steamy style Marilyn Monroe tried on Tony Curtis. She did it with perky joking that distracted his inhibitions and let him relax.

Fun sex and fun drugs—that was the London scene in the early '60s. Judy was digging Lenny Bruce and Mort Sahl records, experimenting with marijuana, enjoying her lovers, taking prescription tranquilizers and sleep aids. She was a hit in *The Boyfriend*, and from there came to America for *Fair Exchange*, a sitcom from the Desilu Studios.

This fresh and energetic sweetheart of the '60s was immediately the darling of the studio—and a target for an aging

Nothing happened next—at least, not between Desi and Judy. There wasn't much chemistry between the London lady and the Latino. Not long after, though, she met a part-Indian actor named Burt Reynolds and the chemistry was there right from the beginning, like mixing H_2 and SO_4.

Judy and Burt met on a plane trip to Florida. Judy was promoting *Fair Exchange* and he was talking up his continuing role on *Gunsmoke*. After the five-hour ride, they felt like they'd known each other all their lives. That night the frisky couple decided to take a tumble together.

At the hotel that night, they lost no time at all. As Judy described it in her book, "We immediately made love. I was engulfed by him, my small body lost in his large frame. He paid scrupulous attention to my sexual desires, sending passionate chills through me. It was a unique encounter for me because we mixed our passion with laughter—an exhilarating combination."

Once again, the love-in was combined with a laugh-in. Burt was a fun guy who loved to imitate Jonathan Winters and recite memorized Winters routines. The only trouble was that once Burt got serious about Judy, he was seriously disturbed by her fun-loving ways. If she was to be Mrs. Burt Reynolds, she had to act like a lady, stop using curse words, wear more conservative dresses, and let her hair grow from pixie to real woman. Jealousy and anger would cross his face whenever he thought about the other guys who had come before him. And when he went out with "the boys" and watched

stag films—and Judy suggested that he bring some films home so they could turn on together—he was repulsed by her lewdness.

It was Burt who wanted the legitimacy of marriage. They had been living together for months when they finally did wed. He was very serious and very romantic about it. He felt the groom should not see the bride before the wedding—or even the night before. He wanted the excitement of a real honeymoon night, a newness, a romantic tension that could only be there if they had not been intimate for a while.

It was a golden honeymoon night for the two of them. Judy would later write, "I was mesmerized by his eyes as they stared directly into mine during our lovemaking. I saw in them the purest love I had ever known as we celebrated the supreme commitment we had just made to each other—marriage."

But soon they were a typical married couple. It wasn't the swinging '60s at all. Burt lay around on the weekends watching football games. When Burt was written out of *Gunsmoke* he couldn't find work. He couldn't even find his hairline—at twenty-six he was going bald. The actor became moody and mean. Meanwhile his plucky wife became the breadwinner. She was now in a sitcom, *The Baileys of Balboa*, a fairly inept little show about veteran comic actor Paul Ford's attempts to keep his boat afloat. The first episode was about bass fishing, and what kind of bait to use to catch a whopper. Judy, occasionally outfitted in a bikini, was around as a love interest for Paul's son, played by Les Brown, Jr.

When Judy would come home, there was Burt, sarcastically wondering if she was spending her free time getting quickies from the film crew. Petty arguments turned violent. "Sure I got slapped and stuff," says Judy, "but it wasn't wife beating. It wasn't *The Burning Bed.* But it wasn't fun. After every explosion there were tears and reconciliation. But after every reconciliation there was another explosion."

She remembers, "There was a bad, knock-down drag-out thing and I got hurt. I went to a neighbor and stayed the night. Then I called Burt the next day. I said, sort of flip like, 'Well maybe we oughta get a divorce.' And he says, 'Well, if that's what you want.' And I'm going 'Ohhhh, God!' Because I really didn't want a divorce."

Bruised by the physical attacks of her immature macho man, tormented by insomnia and sleepwalking, Judy found herself becoming attracted to another woman. Alarmed, but still very much the '60s swinging freethinker, Judy decided to see how strong the attraction was, and whether it was mutual.

It was. They went home one night, danced, held each other close, and kissed. She wrote, "She gently touched and caressed my body, knowing intuitively how to satisfy me. It was a revelation to feel so safe, to be in the hands of a sensitive woman. There was no threat, no invasion. After that night together, we were inseparable."

She says now, "It's nothing to be ashamed of. I was saved by my relationships with women at a time when I needed it most." Judy's nights were spent indulging in "forbidden" love. But during the day, it was all-American girl-boy love. Judy was now filming *Love on a Rooftop,* a new ABC sitcom.

Love on a Rooftop presented Peter Deuel and Judy Carne as David and Julie, a pair of squeaky-clean newlyweds. Judy may have been a British lesbian offscreen, but she put on a good American accent for the show, and looked like she really was in love with Peter Deuel. The show followed *That Girl,* suggesting the kind of adorable bliss Marlo Thomas could have if she could convince Ted Bessel to tie the knot.

Deuel knew of Judy's lesbianism and was understanding but confused, since they were having such a good time kissing and cuddling on the show. Like a sitcom dream come true, *Love on a Rooftop*'s stars fell in love. For a while, Judy vacillated between the two lovers, but then drifted closer to Peter. Ironically, the sincere chemistry between the two didn't spark much confidence at ABC. The show was dropped. Judy and Peter parted.

Judy joined the cast of *Laugh-In,* the most outrageous, countercultural comedy the '60s had seen. A product of a producer known as "C. F. G." Schlatter (it stood for "Crazy Fucking George"), the show was full-tilt insanity. Schlatter encouraged the cast to ad-lib, to think up all kinds of wild and crazy stunts. And Judy, that perky, mischievous little pixie, became the producer's favorite.

Judy became the "sock it to me" girl, doing anything for a laugh. Her catchphrase, a feverish cry of "Sock it to me, sock it to me, sock it to me," was met by explosions of water, tomatoes in the face, and trapdoor falls. She was the swinging, teasing little thing who danced in a tiny bikini with graffiti painted all over her body. Though Judy insisted her breasts were more like "fried eggs," audiences went wild when they saw her. Like Diana Rigg in *The Avengers*, her personality "fleshed out" the fantasy, making an attractive figure seem absolutely smashing. While Barbara Eden had fought the battle of the navel—and lost—Judy was proud to have given America its first televised glimpse of a sexy belly button at work. Even if most of the time it was painted with a bull's-eye.

Another of Judy's shticks was playing a talking "Judy Doll." The catchphrase when men played with this mechanical sexy doll: "Hello, I'm your Judy Doll. Touch my little body—and I hit!"

It was all good, silly, sexy fun. Judy was having a ball. Her best friends were Goldie Hawn and Henry Gibson. Through the first few seasons, *Laugh-In* was fresh, funny, and inventive. It was TV's number-1 show in 1970.

Schlatter took special delight in pushing the censors to the wall. For the "sock it to me" gag, Judy donned a bald cap. When she was pelted so hard her wig came off, she coyly announced, "I've never been bald before!" By the time the censors got it, the show had already aired. Another time, Judy was pelted with water during yet another "sock it to me" scene, partially exposing her breasts through her gown. Schlatter snuck the scene in, delighted that America could see a nipple on national television.

Off-camera Judy occasionally showed her rebellious, revolutionary streak. When she was refused admittance to 21 because she was wearing pants, she simply took them off, creating an instant uproar.

Yes, it was a wild time. But how many times could a girl shout "Sock it to me" and get trashed? Another catchphrase on the show was the "The Flying Fickle Finger of Fate." And fatefully, the *Laugh-In* laugh lifestyle was not all laughs. The dizzying high of the first few seasons was matched by a fearful low. Judy began to see Goldie Hawn's therapist. Her insomnia and need for drugs to combat it increased. Most members of the *Laugh-In* cast were becoming disenchanted. Several left, and as the '60s came to an end, so did Judy's association with *Laugh-In*.

The '60s went out with a blast. Judy hosted a pot party on New Years Eve 1970 that featured special guest Jim Morrison. But after the blast came the tremors and the collapse.

The '70s was a lost decade for Judy. A hoped-for marriage fizzled. She found someone else, married him, and has regretted it ever since. The two of them sank deep into drugs, and when they finally divorced, he was the type of man who demanded that she pay *him* alimony. Her career stalled when audiences, impatiently awaiting "sock it to me" gags, forgot that she had been—and still was—a fine singer and dancer. Her biggest newspaper write-up for a club appearence came when a drunk in the audience "socked it" to her by drenching her with a drink.

He wasn't the only one. More than once a good-natured or well-meaning fan would give her a wallop or splatter her with a glass of water, shouting a gleeful, "Sock it to me! Sock it to me!"

With the "help" of managers and accountants, Judy's savings dwindled to practically nothing. Her agents couldn't get her work. She managed parts in a few musicals—but the few highs were matched by more and more lows. She met a fellow rebel, Steve McQueen, and the two had a torrid but very brief encounter. Her ex-lover Peter Deuel, the sensitive actor with high hopes in the '60s, now renamed Duel, was starring in a TV series called *Alias Smith and Jones*. Until he killed himself.

Judy was surprised when, out of the blue, Burt Reynolds asked her to appear on *The Tonight Show* the night he was guest-hosting. Reynolds, in a replay of their honeymoon night, refused to see her before showtime, the better to create more tension and excitement at the big moment.

"When was the last time we saw each other?" Burt asked.

"Let's see," said Judy. "I think it was when you threw me against the fireplace!"

They shared a chuckle. When Burt asked if Judy had seen his seminude *Cosmopolitan* centerfold, she shot back, "Of course . . . it's terrific. But it's missing your best feature—your arse! He has the most divine little arse!"

Reynolds wondered if she was seeing younger men. Judy said she was. And then she noted that he was seeing older women—an allusion to his then-current romance with Dinah Shore.

"Not older," Reynolds shot back, "just classier."

There were awkward moments, but also ripples of laughter and excitement. Could there be a reconciliation? Judy had hopes. Burt knew he'd made mistakes during the marriage but he wasn't going to try again.

Her professional and private life continued to spiral downward. The harmless druggies that surrounded Judy in the '60s were replaced by hardcore addicts. She was introduced to heroin. Her money ran out. She came to Reynolds begging for five hundred dollars to join a rehab center. She wanted more than the money. She wanted support and love. All Burt could give her was the money. Judy took it, and in her guilt and shame blew it all on more drugs.

In battling her drug problem, Judy looked for any help she could get, reconciling with her ex-husband Robert Bergmann—who still had his own drug problems. When the police discovered his Quaaludes in her apartment, she took the fall. She made headlines in 1977 and 1978 for drug arrests. As the *Miami Herald* reported in 1978, "Carne is facing a string of marijuana, heroin and pill charges from practically one end of the country to the other." She was bitterly discovering what she had heard from Lenny Bruce records—that the only thing worse than an overdose of drugs was an overdose of narcs.

Now nobody wanted to hire the druggie has-been, which made the ordeal worse.

In June 1978, just after her acquittal in one case, she broke her neck in a car accident. Bergmann was behind the wheel, and escaped the wreck without a scratch. Taken half-conscious and half-dead to the hospital, she managed to mutter, "I guess this is the ultimate 'sock it to me.'"

She had to wear a specially constructed cagelike brace attached to her neck and screwed into her skull. About the only good thing about it was that it thrust her back into the headlines—in a sympathetic light. She posed for pictures in the hellish contraption, and described the agony of trying to sleep in it.

Life began again at forty for Judy. She successfully sued her ex-husband for damages caused by the accident and was finally freed of the tormenting brace. She performed in England, playing Elvira in *Blithe Spirit*. In 1985 she wrote her autobiography, *Laughing on the Outside, Crying on the Inside.* She went on tour with it and American audiences were happy to see her. Book reviewers were doubtful. The *Philadelphia Inquirer* wrote with disgust about Judy's "depression; the abuse; the self-abuse; the therapy; the brawls; the flings; the female lovers; the transsexual friends; the brief, stormy second marriage; the betrayals; the heroin addiction; the detoxification and rehabilitation . . . the moronic and almost deadly reunion with her second ex-husband . . . the bad judgment; the bad taste . . ."

She went on *The Regis Philbin Show*, describing her relationship with Burt Reynolds softly saying, "I'm really sort of hoping he'll get in touch . . ." And here was Judy, still admitting "I still am a magnet for trouble," still admitting she needed prescription drugs to go to sleep, and actually acknowledging her delight in still smoking pot: "Oh yeah, yeah."

At the time her book came out, in 1985, Judy was arrested twice, both times for possession of cocaine and pot. Judy was only partially repentant. After all, she told one reporter, what was so bad about a drug problem? "Nowadays, it's like you get on the cover of *People* magazine, you check into the Betty Ford clinic, and you've got a new career."

In an interview with CNN cable TV, she said, "I have no regrets . . . I do see my mistakes. I don't intend to make them again." But in 1986 she made a personal appearance at Cockham Wood Prison. The sentence was three months. She was jeered at by the other inmates, humiliated, and at one point nearly killed by a scissor-wielding tormentress. She was forced to go "cold turkey" with drugs while she scrubbed floors.

In 1987, police confiscated cocaine from her luggage at a London airport. The "sock it to me" girl was socked again. After all this, Judy's luck has to change for the better.

Goldie Hawn

GOOD MORNING WORLD

First broadcast: **September 5, 1967**
Last broadcast: **September 17, 1968**

LAUGH-IN

First broadcast: **January 22, 1968**
Last broadcast: **May 14, 1973**

"L*augh-In* reruns?" Goldie Hawn smiles enigmatically. "I haven't seen them in about two years. I'm so far away from that time of my life now . . . I am different, decidedly different . . . I mean there's nothing that I feel bad about or embarrassed about, it was a great time in television history . . ."

History began when Goldie Jeanne Hawn was born in Takoma Park, Maryland, on November 21, 1945. Her Presbyterian father was a musician, a "funny, sarcastic" man who influenced her sense of humor. Her Jewish mother was "a giving woman. I'm not an entertainer because I need attention I didn't get as a baby. I got plenty . . . I've been a giggler, a laugher, since I was three years old."

Like her *Laugh-In* friend Judy Carne, Goldie took ballet lessons as a child. She grew up learning how to carry herself gracefully, but her boyish figure and indifferent looks caused her a lot of grief during puberty. The boys weren't interested in her at all. If they paid any attention to her, it was to laugh and call her "Goldie-locks."

She tried to change her image in junior high school by "stepping into the school bathroom and putting on falsies and eight slips and a straight skirt so I'd look like I had a shape. And frosted pink lipstick. And all this black stuff on my eyes." She didn't look dangerous; just silly. She tried the other extreme, becoming a cheer-leader. Still she had little to cheer about: "I wasn't very well developed physically. Mine was a more difficult adolescence than most girls have. I never went out very much."

Goldie appeared in school productions and branched out into local summer stock. At eighteen, the slender young ac-tress played Juliet in *Romeo and Juliet,* and suddenly everything clicked. The production was held outside in an amphi-theater and three thousand people showed up. They applauded her wildly, and not even a sudden downpour could drive them away.

Goldie attended American University, but didn't last more than a year. She came to New York in 1964 to become a star. Audiences loved her—as a go-go dancer in cheap bars. "One of the customers, sit-ting a few yards in front of me, unzipped his zipper. And he began to expose him-self. I kept looking away. The other guys were howling. I was in a den of perverts . . . I was so frightened I ran out of the place."

She had to keep coming back to the clubs in order to pay the rent. Her life consisted of sweating out nights dancing in front of fierce-eyed men, and waiting out days in a slum apartment filled with fiercer-eyed rats.

She was working with, and living with, "the dregs of society, having both men and women relate to me purely as a sexual creature, coming on to me, propositioning me." The sweet young thing from Mary-land learned that the Broadway area of Manhattan festered with peep shows, whores, and con artists. In New York, a classically trained dancer had to work strip clubs. She moved to Las Vegas—where she worked all night long in a cho-rus line. That was worse.

Finally Goldie moved to California. There was no shortage of dancers there. All she could get was a job in the chorus for an Andy Griffith variety special. But Hollywood loved cute blondes with a kooky streak. She was perfect for sitcoms. Goldie played Sandy in *Good Morning World,* with Joby Baker and Ronnie Schell as fun-loving morning disc jockeys. One of the few who watched that show was George Schlatter, who was casting *Laugh-In.*

George didn't want stand-up comics, he wanted talented comic actors and ac-tresses. He found Goldie. To him she was a natural. And what Schlatter wanted was natural humor. His pioneering style on *Laugh-In* was to keep things loose, to keep the cameras rolling, to encourage ad-libbing. He wanted his performers to be themselves. The cameras kept rolling when the twenty-two-year-old Goldie stumbled over her lines and stared into

♥ **Gigglin' Goldie and Solid Goldie**—a cutie pose from *Seems Like Old Times*, and some elegance in her first TV special, coming off her *Laugh-In* success.

the camera with a sweet look of confusion. The relaxed atmosphere was perfect for bringing out Goldie's warm, fun-loving giggle and silly ad-libs.

Even before *Laugh-In*, the excitement and tension of performing sometimes produced the unexpected. "Once I did pee on stage," she admits. "I was in the chorus of *Kiss Me Kate*. We were in Springfield, Massachusetts, and one of the actors was playing a strong man . . . but the strong man couldn't find his loincloth at the last minute, so he showed up in a girl's leotard. I laughed so hard I peed down my leg. It was visible from the light booth, so you knew everyone could see it."

On *Laugh-In*, Goldie was almost totally exposed. She parlayed her stage fright and nervousness into giggles and bloopers. Often she was stripped down to a flimsy bikini, just like the "sock it to me" girl, her friend Judy Carne. Goldie's five-foot-six, 118-pound body was very boyish, like Judy's, but when she donned her bikini it didn't seem to matter. As she danced around, comical graffiti all over her body, she exuded good humor spiced with an innocent, fun-loving sexuality.

Goldie wasn't just another "dumb blonde." She had personality. Her first biographer, Connie Berman, explains it this way: "That leggy, kewpie-eyed, blond doll . . . was cute, with just the right amount of a Lolita-brand sexiness. She was the kind of girl you could present happily to mother with pride and then sneak around for a roll in the hay when no one was looking."

George Schlatter agrees with Connie: "You don't know whether to take her to bed or take her home to your mother."

She was sweet and silly, but she was also vulnerable. She was obviously flustered when she turned her lines into bloopers, and Schlatter made sure she stayed that way by deliberately switching the cue cards around and putting surprise dirty words on them to break her up.

But after a while, the practical jokes began to seem more like an assault. Her giggling was from nervousness as much as childlike delight. Her breaking up was really a sign of breaking down. One day Goldie had to do a stunt jump—and she nearly jumped over the line. The stage crew was shocked by the sight of the trembling, tearful Goldie. It was only after some soothing words from Judy Carne that she could continue.

"I can't really call it a nervous breakdown," she says today. "I was just beginning, the rise to success had just started. It was the most frightening thing that ever happened to me."

Goldie knew she couldn't continue that way. The anxiety attacks were hell. She was a nervous wreck. Her body rebelled. She recalls now, "I was unable to walk into a public place without throwing up."

The giggling *Laugh-In* girl without a care in the world went into therapy. Gradually a lot of the symptoms of her fears and insecurities began to disappear. And the "Goldie Hawn" character—the simpleminded giggler—disappeared, too. Goldie ditched *Laugh-In* and went into the movies.

Goldie had been nominated for an Emmy, for Best Variety Performance, competing with Ruth Buzzi, Harvey Korman, and Arte Johnson. The two men tied and won. But the next year Goldie and Arte won for Special Individual Achievement.

In the movies, the awards came even quicker. She won an Oscar for Best Supporting Actress for her very first film,

Cactus Flower. The competition was tremendous: Sylvia Miles in *Midnight Cowboy*, Susannah York in *They Shoot Horses, Don't They?*, and Dyan Cannon in *Bob & Carol & Ted & Alice*. (Technically, this was her second film—she had a small part in a 1968 Disney movie, *The One and Only Genuine Original Family Band*. She was barely onscreen long enough to giggle—or get to know the film's star, Kurt Russell.)

As Goldie's star was on the rise her marriage was falling apart. Her husband, Gus Trikonis, had been a dancer in New York, more successful at it than Goldie, making it to Broadway in the musical *Bajour*.

Goldie's Greek was not her first. "I've gone with four Greeks in my life," she said at the time, "I don't know what it is that brings us together so often. I really think I'm a reincarnated Greek."

They married in 1969, during Goldie's stressful last year with *Laugh-In*. She'd hoped that the marriage would strengthen their relationship. She believed in marriage. "I want to be married," she explained. "I want an honest relationship with a man. I don't want to be some kind of half-baked floozy who lives with whatever man interests her for the present, then goes on to another."

While Goldie bloomed in California, Gus did not. She had *Laugh-In* and he was more of a shut-in. She made the money. He couldn't get his career started, and he couldn't stop her from her next role—which included a nude scene.

Nude scenes were still controversial in 1970, and there was always a debate over their validity. As it turned out, Goldie had some concerns about it, too. *There's a Girl in My Soup* was important to her—she admired Peter Sellers and was delighted to see a master at work. But was the nude scene important?

"I was getting out of bed and putting on a coat and the director finessed me into doing it nude. There was absolutely no reason on earth for me to get out of that bed naked. Roy Boulting, the director, told me he'd clear the set and he really played on my insecurities, making me feel that it was my duty as an actress to trust him. I gave in . . ."

No wonder her next role was so different—in *$* she played a deceptively bright and cunning character who could cut through men like butter.

More important parts followed, including *Butterflies Are Free* and *Shampoo*. The latter was an attempted satire of hedonism and leering swingers, but it was cowritten by leering swinger Warren Beatty. Viewers could leer at the shots of Goldie in a baby doll nightie, waving her legs back and forth, exposing her speckled panties. The film never took much of a stand. "We're always tryin' to nail 'em and they don't like it," an actor says of women. "They like it and they don't like it." Goldie liked Beatty, but not enough to get serious with him.

The chemistry was much better in *The Duchess and the Dirt Water Fox*, where the relaxed, likable George Segal was a foil for the deceptively bright duchess. Judith Crist, in *Saturday Review*, announced,

Outrageously funny—Goldie in
The Duchess and the Dirtwater
Fox.

"Hawn, allowed at long last to display her song and dance talents along with her gift as actress and . . . delicious sexpot, is just a joy to watch."

Others took over the role of dumb TV blonde. Suzanne Somers became a superstar on *Three's Company.* At the time, Goldie remarked, "That girl is sexy, dumb, vacant. I felt that my character was much more joyous, less stupid, perhaps more frivolous. She had a kind of youthful naïveté and femininity. The laugh was not from a sexual place, but from surprise, zest. It was just different. I don't think this girl was aware of sex at all. There was a purity to her."

Into the '70s, Goldie dropped one husband—and found another. The shaky marriage to Trikonis had ended in separation in 1972. They were divorced in 1975.

Today, Trikonis reflects, "Her success became an incredible threat to my ego. Goldie tried her best to deal with it, but she had to flex her muscles. She said, 'I have to get on with what I'm doing.' And I said, 'Well, that's fine. I'll be around.' But it sort of ended."

The end of Trikonis dragged out for years. But it only took a few hours for Goldie to meet and become intrigued with Bill Hudson, her second husband. As in the case of Judy Carne and Burt Reynolds, the relationship began during a long plane ride. Only a few months later Goldie was expecting Bill's baby. She was six months pregnant when the two got married in 1976. "Being a mother is the greatest experience of my life," she said. Goldie's second child arrived in 1979, and as far as the public knew, she was happy in her domestic bliss.

The '60s sweetheart entered the '80s as one of the "twenty-five most intriguing people" in a *People* magazine cover story. In private life she was married with two kids. On the screen, she and Chevy Chase made a delightful duo in *Foul Play*, which brought her into the '80s with a box-office hit.

Once again, Goldie's career was on the upswing. And once again, her husband's career was headed down. In the past, Bill Hudson and his Hudson Brothers had hit records. Goldie's attempt at singing had been a failure. But now the Hudson Brothers were history. And so was the marriage.

"This is the most painful thing I've ever gone through," Goldie said when divorce proceedings began in 1981. She once more had to examine what marriage was all about: "A true marriage should be about love and sharing a life together, sharing art and walks and quiet moments . . . not going out to a disco, drinking a bottle of champagne and finding yourself in love, madly, with someone you just met . . . loving someone is very different and places a lot of responsibility on you. None of it has much to do with romantic dreams."

Her personal life was in a shambles, but the public saw the other side. They saw *Private Benjamin,* a superhit that has grossed over seventy million dollars. Goldie was nominated for a Best Actress Oscar, but lost to Sissy Spacek for *Coal Miner's Daughter*. She followed that film with *Seems Like Old Times*, and that was followed by a *Time* magazine cover story. "If Goldie Hawn is a dumb blonde, Henry Kissinger is a dopey brunet," *Time* wrote. "At thirty-five, this former go-go girl's back-to-back successes have made her the most popular actress in the country."

As a producer, Goldie was able to exert tremendous control over her movies. It wasn't that hard for her to get that position of power—studios had confidence in her ability to make successful comedies. But even the light stuff had to be the right stuff. "I'm a woman now," she said. "Not a sexy nymphet. I think I used to be a cross between a puritanical angel and a nymphet. I was young and naïve. I'm different now."

Onscreen, she showed the difference, balancing ditz and feminism, vulnerability and responsibility. In *Protocol*, she played a cocktail waitress forced to don a feathery Emu outfit (a ludicrous

♥ **Busy businesswoman and superstar: Goldie is an expert in *Protocol*.**

parody of the Playboy bunny look). Shot in the backside while foiling an assassination attempt on a Middle Eastern big shot, she becomes a celebrity. "Can you be that dumb and run for office?" a politician wonders. After some adventures, parties, tough situations, and consciousness raising, she is ready to run for Congress—and win. "Before I started to work for the government I never read the Constitution. The Declaration of Independence . . . it's about we the people. And that's me . . . all of us . . ."

Some critics objected to the preaching, and the idea of Goldie saving the entire country. In her next film, she only had to salvage a football team. In *Wildcats* she played the tough-talking female football coach who gets the position over male protests ("Do you know how to get good penetration?" she asks a fellow teacher). As Janet Maslin of *The New York Times* wrote, "This is another of the iron buttercup roles in which Miss Hawn has been specializing since *Private Benjamin*, films in which her inspired dizziness masks an unexpectedly strong will."

Goldie actually went to ex–football coach John Sanders for instruction. "It wasn't enough for her to learn the game," he recalls. She learned "to master the moves, call the plays and speak football lingo as though she knew exactly what she was talking about."

She also knew what she was talking about when reporters asked her about Kurt Russell. Five years younger than Goldie, Kurt got to know her when they did *Swing Shift* in 1984. An actor on the set told Russell, "The thing about Goldie that'll surprise you is her figure." Specifically, her delightful rear. Kurt looked and had to agree. But that was just the beginning, not the end.

"We're as married as two people can be," says Goldie. "I cannot stand the marriage laws. They are archaic. It's all about big business. You know if marriages don't work out it can really ruin your life . . . I'm not saying that at some time or another we just might not tie the knot, but for the moment my memories of marriage have not been very good."

Russell had been married too, and had a son with actress Season Hubley.

Goldie and Kurt's son Wyatt was born in 1986. The parents now live on a giant ranch in Old Snowmass, Colorado. They love it up there. "A great place to raise the kids," as Goldie says, including the ones from her previous marriage. In Colorado, Kurt rides around in the tractor Goldie gave him for his birthday, and supervises the alfalfa they're raising. Goldie has learned how to cook some of the animals Kurt hunts, and has even made a good elk stew. On David Letterman's show, the host was appalled that Goldie was living with guns around the house, and that Kurt was a hunter. But Goldie said, "I think it's great. I would never do it myself—ever—but it's something he grew up with. Kurt's almost half American Indian." They have sheep, horses, and used to have a pig—until it was slaughtered and eaten. Goldie gives an apologetic giggle over that.

They lead, in Kurt's words, an "extraordinarily ordinary" lifestyle. Goldie gave a few tips on an enduring relationship in an interview on the Oprah Winfrey show: "Loving someone is easy, it happens fast . . . you're caught up with the thrust of it, it's sexy, it's exciting, but all of a sudden this great illusion that you've built begins to crumble . . . the key is not to create the illusion. It's to just go in there and understand the things that make you happy and how to make him happy and all the little differences you have don't count. I don't argue with him. Expectation is a very dangerous thing."

The ranch is paradise. About the only sign of stress is that Goldie still smokes a few cigarettes too many. Sure, she occasionally gets depressed, but not more than anybody else. And when she does, she isn't afraid to feel her own pain. "I'm not a person who wants to get out of their depression. It's a moment of reflection. A moment of growth for me. Eventually I'll do something good because of it. A lot of my creative work comes out of those moments."

In 1987 she made *Overboard,* another familiar and accessible comedy. As Goldie says, "I'm not gonna move a mountain . . . you've got so much time to live your life. . . . Do what you want to do. . . . We entertain, and we have a blast at doing it." Kurt played a carpenter abused by "useless, empty, nail-polishing, toe-polishing, rich bitch" Goldie. She learned her lesson. "I learn—or she learns—the power of love and the importance of it, and how the collecting of things is not as important as giving."

She continues to balance the big business of moviemaking and producing her own films with the business of raising a family. On *PM Magazine,* in March of 1986, she explained, "I'm as liberated as anybody . . . but my home and my children are still the most important."

Interviewers looking for the Tweety-bird lookalike with the big blue eyes have to look elsewhere now. In person, Goldie bears very little relation to that meekly giggling cutie she was on *Laugh-In.* She's matured, her face has developed character. It's very possible that before too long, the zany comedy roles will be permanently at an end, and dramatic parts, or character comedy, will prevail.

Though living and working with the same man is a dangerous thing to attempt, Goldie insists that there's no problem so far spending twenty-four hours a day with Kurt Russell. "While we were making the picture, both of us would wake up in the morning and we'd go to work, and always enjoy that. And then if he had to go to work before I did, it was just not as much fun—when he was working without me and vice versa. And we would always express that to each other—that it isn't as much fun when we're not together. I hope it lasts forever."

Is there anything Goldie feels she's missing in her life now? What does she want? "The scary part," she says with a grin, "is I pretty much have it."

♥ Goldie's gone from the single swinger image . . . to *Swing Shift* and other movies with husband Kurt Russell.

Barbara Feldon

GET SMART

First broadcast: September 18, 1965
Last broadcast: September 11, 1970

She was the sultry spy on *Get Smart*, and she was the sultry sex symbol in '60s TV commercials, selling hair tonic to "*grrrrrrr* . . . tigers!*" But Barbara Feldon never took it that seriously. In a gallery of '60s sweethearts, she can point herself out right away: "I'm the girl with the drooping eyelids. That sultry gaze is mostly myopia, I'm afraid."

Born Barbara Hall, March 12, 1939 (the date has often been given as 1941), she grew up in Pittsburgh. Her father sold cardboard boxes. She characterizes her childhood as "lonely," and remembers

Pittsburgh with smoky solemnity, a place where "at ten in the morning the cars had their headlights on. At noon the sun was just an orange glow in the sky. And your wrists were always dirty."

Her first brush with show business was at six when she played the triangle in the school band and had her own little solo. In seventh grade she took up the French horn ("because it sounded lacy and feminine") and later took dancing lessons. She began appearing in school plays. The young woman may have been "too tall" for the boys at Bethel High, but on stage the talent behind the tallness interested everyone in the audience.

She graduated from Carnegie Institute of Technology as a drama major. Most of her training was useful, but not all. "College was worthwhile, it takes you out of your environment, but those acting classes—spending all that time pretending to be a banana. . . ."

When she came to New York she managed to land a part in *Caligula*. But, "It was a crawl-on. All I did was crawl on stage and eat some grapes." She wasn't only eating grapes. Barbara enjoyed food, building 145 pounds onto her five-foot-eight frame. "She was stacked," recalls ex-husband Lucien Verdoux Feldon. They met at a Carnegie Hall concert in 1958. He called her "Pussy Cat" and she called him "Muggin." She appeared in the chorus of a *Ziegfeld Follies* show starring Bea Lillie, but earned her biggest paycheck taking time off from the show to compete on *The $64,000 Question*.

TV audiences were astounded that the beauty was brainy. Her category? Shakespeare. Her winnings? The full $64,000.

Barbara and her husband opened their own art gallery, "filled with hostile paintings and hostile people," but it flopped. He found work as a photographer's representative and that helped Barbara gain entry into the exclusive world of modeling. But once she gained entry, she just stood there. "The two top model agencies told me I'd never make a model—thin-faced girls were in, and I have a full face." Her figure was full and curvy. She shed nearly forty pounds in order to present a more willowy figure. She managed to find work with designer Pauline Trigére.

She learned a model's discipline: "I weighed only 107 then. I adjusted my thinking about food and came to enjoy low-calorie, nutritious foods. I could get rhapsodic over a ripe pear."

When she first moved to commercials, "A commercial producer said he wouldn't even turn his camera on to test me, because nobody would buy anything I sold." Fortunately others disagreed. Her first parts were strange. She wore only a towel for a deodorant ad, and for another "I was rolled up in a carpet. It took forty takes to get that right. For another one, I soaked in a tub of hot water for eight hours. I came out looking like a white prune."

Her big break was a Top Brass hair tonic commercial, where she lay on a tigerskin rug and whispered, "I want a word with all you tigers . . . grrrr, I like you . . ." That was enough. If smearing some goo on your head would make Barbara like you—well, sales for the product doubled. "I was so soft-sell, I just kind of whispered. And I was tongue-in-cheek. I haven't had my tongue out of my cheek in years. It was right-time-at-the-right-place. I was suddenly in vogue." The commercial was spoofing corny '50s "bachelor apartment" sexuality, but it had a sensuality of its own.

She recalls that the sexy "grrrr" was real acting. "You have to do it in the back of your throat, with your uvula."

Columnists began turning on to the sexy young star. Sidney Skolsky told his panting readers, "She sleeps in a huge bed . . . she seldom wears a nightgown, never pajamas."

Barbara came to California to act. "Oh, I attracted much attention. After all, I was the girl with 'sex appeal' and my words, 'Sic 'em tiger' became popular throughout the country. But when it came to acting, well, I found the doors closed to me." George C. Scott was the one who smashed the barriers. He cast her for a lead role in an episode of his *East Side, West Side* series. She followed it with *Profiles in Courage* and an episode of *The Nurses.*

Lamont Johnson, who directed the *Nurses* episode, said at the time, "There is almost nothing right with her personally; one eye droops, her legs are skinny, she has buck teeth. But she radiates something marvelous. She is innately chic, so all these things combine to make her physical problems assets. The combination will make her a star."

Barbara played in *The Man from U.N.C.L.E.* and *Mr. Broadway.* Ironically it was the latter, where she happened to play an industrial spy, that drew the attention of Buck Henry and Mel Brooks. "We had no special comedian in mind for Smart," says Henry. "We wrote dialogue suitable for any stand-up comedian. But we had our eyes on . . . Barbara." They used her in the black-and-white pilot episode and were hooked. The following 137 episodes would be in color.

"You know," she says, "I had to be talked into doing the pilot of *Get Smart.* At first, I said absolutely no. I wanted no part of living in California away from my husband. But I was intrigued by the fact that Agent 99 didn't have a name." She went from sexy roles and drama into comedy.

"Dramatic acting can be great but you can't spend the whole day weeping in your bandages," she says. "Comedy has a pace and a style to it. You can improvise

like musicians. I love the energy and vitality of it . . . I remember being in a bad mood one day. So I went to a Mae West festival and I laughed so much I came out feeling better."

She added humor to her sexy secret agent by "a kind of wink at the audience without being so obvious as to do it. At the same time, I performed as honestly as I could."

Of Agent 99 she recalls, "This was about the time Betty Friedan's book *[The Feminine Mystique]* came out. Agent 99 really was not a subservient kind of character. She was demonstrably more intelligent than Max. In the script—I'm not talking about Don Adams. She had dignity and style. She was a caricature in a sense, but I'm not embarrassed in any way that I played Agent 99."

Agent 99's smarts were smarter than Smart's in many episodes. There was one where the robot Hymie must win a race, but stalls at the finish line. She's the one who brilliantly grabs Max's shoe phone and coaxes the robot across using the phone's magnetism. (That episode, incidentally, featured a broad parody of *The Avengers,* with villains named Snead and Mrs. Neal.)

Agent 99 was sensuous; Max was not. Many of the jokes, especially during the first few seasons, were aimed at Max's peculiar ambivalence toward his sultry partner. Here was a guy who, when looking at a bruise on his right ankle, petulantly told her, "Turn your head!" In another episode, 99 must stay over at his apartment to guard him from a KAOS hit squad.

"But you're a girl!" Max whines. "What would my mother think?"

He finally relents as long as 99 stays in a separate bedroom. When she begins watching his movements via a closed-circuit TV system, he refuses to even take his shirt off, crying "You're invading my privacy. Not to mention my modesty!"

She answers, "I've seen your Adam's apple before. It's cute."

Agent 99 was always very indulgent of Max. Her tolerance included putting up with one of the longest-running jokes in sitcom history. Just one of the series:

"They won't take me alive and don't tell me they want me dead."

"They want you dead."

"I asked you not to tell me that!"

Whether it was "Would you believe . . ." or "I asked you not to tell me that," or "Missed it by that much," or his insistence on using "the Cone of Silence" at the office and "the Cube of Safety" in his living room, 99 never lost her patience. It didn't even matter that he never called her anything but a number.

Female viewers could admire 99—she could take care of herself in moments of danger. She even shot and killed KAOS agents; remarkable for a woman on a sitcom. She used mental resources too, and she was alluring without ever being a stereotypical sex symbol.

Though Barbara didn't do many stunts on the show, she was more than prepared. In high school she had been on the basketball and touch football teams, and was an excellent swimmer and horseback rider. On the show, many believed that

♥ **Demure but delightful: Barbara's typical smart get-up.**

the tall, good-natured 99 was a mother figure to the short, childlike Max. Young male viewers could imagine themselves partnered with this nonthreatening, supportive, willing woman. Most any male could imagine himself netting 99—since they had to feel superior to Max, the little man with the mismatched ears, beady eyes, and laughable voice.

As 99, some of Barbara's shy, vulnerable traits showed through. She tended to cast her eyes down demurely when embarrassed or trying not to criticize Max, her plump lower lip pursing almost like a child's. She never flaunted her figure, which often was encased in long-sleeved dresses with modest hemlines. It was achingly funny—or just plain aching—to see 99 waste her affection on oblivious Max:

"Oh Max, you're so brave, so dedicated, so wonderful!"

"I understand, 99, I feel the same way."

"Then say it, Max, say it."

"I'm brave and dedicated and wonderful!"

Though the show was being broadcast during the height of the era of psychedelia and sex revolution, *Get Smart* rarely reflected its time. Max was as square as *Dragnet*'s Joe Friday. A few late episodes featured encounters with hippies, or KAOS agents staked out at a disco, but generally the show avoided confronting the new generation. Agent 99 got away with a quick frug on the dance floor now and then, but she wasn't swinging, either.

At the time a reporter asked Barbara about the hippie movement. "Of course," she said, "there are extremists in such a movement, I feel alarmed by LSD and that sort of thing. But I watch them without hostility, only with curiosity, because something is happening although I don't quite know what."

Don Adams and Barbara Feldon were no gossip item. As she pointed out at the time, "The show is Don Adams. Without him, nothing. My softness, sincerity, gullibility and loving despair are simply a foil for his brittle vitality. As for our relationship off-screen, I adore him, I feel af-

fection for him, but I don't know him. We are of another world." The ex-Marine who had put in many tough years as a nightclub comic didn't socialize much with Barbara. Barbara preferred to unwind from her work by gazing at the stars through her telescope and quietly exploring the beach for sea shells.

She obtained a Mexican divorce from her husband Lucien in 1967. She lived with her Siamese cat, Yang. Barbara told Sidney Skolsky that astronomy was her prime hobby, though she dabbled in needlework, painting, and poetry. "I'm so fascinated with how beautiful it is out there—astronomy has affected my whole philosophy of life. Among the planets and stars, some 30 trillion miles apart, we on earth are all that's human—and you suddenly feel humans are fascinating."

In the world of sitcoms, *Get Smart* had just about reached the end of its run. For several years the show had been fresh and inventive. It had risen as high as number 12 in the ratings for 1966. Barbara was nominated for Emmy awards two years in a row, but lost to Lucille Ball and then to Hope Lange for *The Ghost and Mrs. Muir.* The show featured all kinds of fun guest stars, from Carol Burnett and Don Rickles to a continuing role for Bernie Koppell's inane KAOS villain Siegfried. The show expanded to include Dick Gautier as Hymie the robot and Dave Ketchum as Agent 13, the guy always given embarrassing surveillance assignments in mailboxes and under potted plants. There were *Get Smart* toys (including a miniature camera and crystal radio in a pen), and Barbara even recorded a pair of songs for RCA—"a female baritone, sort of a torchy number" called "Max," and on the flip side, "99." But trying to make it into the '70s, the formula began wearing thin.

The show was canceled by NBC. CBS decided to rescue it, and switch the emphasis from now-stale villains and violence to domestic comedy. Max and 99 were going to get married! But Maxwell Smart was still Maxwell Smart. And 99 was still exasperated:

"Max, we're getting married in a few weeks. I've already sent out the wedding invitations—"

"Are you sure? I didn't get one."

Max and 99 got married on November 16, 1970. Agent 99's bridesmaid on the show was Dorothy Adams—Don's wife.

The wedding was a happy occasion, but not for viewers. The show, getting more predictable, really lost steam. There was none of the gently steaming sexual tension between 99 and Smart that was very much a part of the show before. Max called 99 "darling" now, and she called Max "sweetheart." For viewers, the wedding was an anticlimax. Agent 99 was now officially Max's, Max was still pretty much of an idiot, and 99 was foolish for not having saved herself for someone better.

Even if she was the perfect housewife and cook, it didn't matter. The Chief comes over for dinner, and 99 announces, "All we're having is artichokes vinaigrette, fresh baby shrimp, vichyssoise and beef Wellington."

Max grimaces. "Well, he'll just have to take pot luck." Then he's annoyed be-cause there's no dessert. "Well, why don't you serve the vichyssoise as dessert and tell him it was potato ice cream that melted."

Soon 99 was even burdened with babies.

None of this seemed to bother Barbara, who stayed calm, relaxed, and in control no matter what was going on with *Get Smart*. Coworkers remember her being very similar to 99 in her easygoing style. She admits, "When I work I'm very relaxed. I don't cause trouble. I'm not highstrung. I tend to be a listener. I'm mostly not aware of myself, but of what's happening or other people."

The others on the show had the tension. The late Edward Platt (the Chief of Control) was a "sweet man," but tense. He had suffered a heart attack before the show—and died of a heart attack shortly after it ended. Don Adams was nice to work with, but as the star of the show he had the most to lose. He'd watch the rushes very seriously, while Barbara looked at the day's filming "like home movies," never being very critical.

When Barbara's marriage eroded during *Get Smart*, the main reason was distance. Lucien still lived in New York. Another problem was time. On the show Barbara had to work thirteen hours a day, getting up at six in the morning.

Some time after they divorced, Barbara began living with *Get Smart* producer Burt Nodella, an arrangement that lasted eleven years.

While in California, Barbara had two homes. One was in the Hollywood Hills.

ing assignments, there were none for women. She told Kay Gardella in 1974, "Out of the 25 dramatic shows last year, all starred men. There just aren't any good roles for mature, attractive women. The women who are scoring in TV today, for the most part, are all in comedy."

She was speaking fact, not laying blame. "Too many women are willing write off their lack of success as the fault of men and therefore allow themselves to be defeated. They should be more encouraged and step out and try to do something and not

♥ The dangerous side of 99—Barbara in *Lady Killer*, an ABC TV movie from 1974.

♥ An atypical pose—playing a gypsy on an episode of the quiz show *Don Adams' Screen Test*.

The other was a forty-three-foot cruiser docked at Marina del Rey. It was called *Cioppino*, which is a type of fish stew.

Barbara was not interested in doing another series after *Get Smart*. She wanted "no major responsibilities," she said at the time. Barbara made a few TV movies, and in 1974 starred in a summer replacement show, *Dean Martin's Comedy World*. Her most notable movie was 1975's parody of beauty pageants, *Smile*.

Barbara wasn't smiling when she noticed that, even if she'd wanted challeng-

blame men all the time. I have always found men to be willing helpers and not envious of a woman's success."

As the '70s, ended, Barbara packed up and headed for New York. She'd made money from *Get Smart* but her contract was for a specific number of reruns. Now she no longer shares in the profits. "I'm not complaining," she insists.

She guest-hosted on *A.M. America,* and that led to a half-hour magazine show called *Special Edition,* in 1978, which covered light news items—everything from a profile of "Peanuts" cartoonist Charles Schulz to a segment on skateboarding. *Variety* said Barbara was "a charming and intelligent host," but questioned the show's intelligence.

Barbara looked for other jobs, including voice-overs. But at the time she found that "ninety-three percent of off-camera voices were male." Little things like that began to perk her interest in feminism. She began to work for feminist causes, and joined Norman Lear's wife in raising money for the Equal Rights Amendment.

In 1979, Maxwell Smart returned for *The Nude Bomb,* a theatrical feature film. Realizing how long it had taken her to shake the 99 persona, Barbara didn't want to ingrain that image any deeper. Fortunately, she wasn't pressed to come aboard. Max was free to frolic with other female spies—though few viewers seemed inclined to watch. Today Barbara is a bit saddened that *The Nude Bomb* was an "exploitation" that tarnished the image of Maxwell Smart.

Instead of re-hashing *Get Smart,* Bar-

bara made a few TV movies *(Vacation in Hell* and *Before and After)* and entered the new decade by starring on Broadway for the first time, and hosting *The '80s Woman* for the Daytime cable network, a product of Hearst/ABC.

Past Tense was the play she did with Laurence Luckinbill. For Barbara, the best part was finally appearing before a live audience: "That's so wonderful . . . to look at audiences . . . they have real faces. There's something very comforting about the imperfection of masses of people. It makes you comfortable with yourself, because you know how imperfect you are."

The TV show was another challenge. "I don't want to do what I can do easily," she told interviewer Kim Gantz at the time. It was hard to break the stereotype of the sexy Agent 99, but she did. Her show was not the usual afternoon gossip show à la Virginia Graham.

Feldon was one of the first female TV hosts to bring controversy to the air. She had programs about abortion, about women's rights, about legal issues. She was really a logical choice for host: "I do support myself, I do live alone—not really by choice . . . I'd like to meet a lovely man who shares my interests. On the other hand I possibly will not. It's part of the hand you're dealt. It's a challenge—and I'm not atypical."

She told writer Ralph Tyler at the time that "Today's woman doesn't have emotional or financial security. She has to go out and compete within a highly materialistic machine—and because of that

♥ **Talk-show hosting in the '80s.**

she has guilt about both her family and her job—how do you do both? With the opportunity goes a sense of loss . . . It's an interesting time, but it's a difficult time." She recalled her grandmother, and other women of past times who "had spiritual security, emotional security, financial security. She did not have to go out and compete in the world. By and large, she lived more comfortably than women today. Maybe she did not live as fully— that is a question."

Critics praised her, surprised that she could be both "attractive and articulate." The hardest thing for Barbara Feldon was to be like Barbara Walters: "I was brought up being told not to offend anybody."

The show had more than its share of controversy, but like many talk-show hosts, Barbara sometimes found herself questioning the point of all that talk. "I don't sense that people believe in anything," she told reporter Toby Kahn in 1983. "It's more of a holding on and trying not to lose ground."

Many still hold on to their image of Barbara as 99. She says that when she leaves her New York apartment, she's bound to meet a fan or two. "It happens not so often that it makes life difficult and often enough that it makes life very friendly." She mentioned that fans approach her more because she was a TV star, not a movie star. While movie stars are "bigger than life," she notes that TV stars are "more like a friend. We've been in people's living rooms. They've been watching us in their undies. We're . . . like family."

In 1986 Barbara appeared at a press conference with other female members of the Screen Actors Guild, protesting male dominance in voice-over commercials. Barbara reported that ninety percent of voice-over work was still done by males. She insisted "nowhere was there evidence to support the assumption of a woman being less effective as a sales force."

Barbara continues to perform, to conduct poetry readings, and to explore a wide range of hobbies including playing the piano and French horn. "The most interesting thing in life is mastering something that you haven't yet," she says. "It puts you in touch with the people who have mastered it." Stimulating new people and new ideas have kept Barbara Feldon very much a "99"—above the normal, average 98.6.

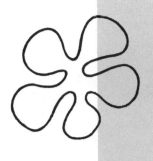

Fantasy Figures

Tina Louise

GILLIGAN'S ISLAND

First broadcast: September 26, 1964
Last broadcast: September 4, 1967

Whoever heard of such a dumb idea for a TV show? Seven castaways stranded on a desert island week after week!

Tina Louise didn't.

She thought *Gilligan's Island* was going to be about the island adventures of movie star Ginger Grant. Most of the other characters didn't even have names. Gilligan and the Skipper were open calls—Jerry Van Dyke and Carroll O'Connor were first choice, later Bob Denver and Alan Hale, Jr. But who cared? The star, she was told, was Tina Louise.

Tina *was* a star, even then. No one else in the cast had been a major news item for nearly a decade—for scandals, society-page gossip, magazine pictorials, and movie and Broadway roles. Nobody else in the cast had been photographed as often, or treated like such royalty.

Take *The New York Times*—they announced *Gilligan's Island* with the headline TV SHOW FOR TINA LOUISE.

About the only time Tina didn't make headlines was when she was born, February 11, 1934. She was Tina Blacker then, the daughter of a Brooklyn candy store owner, a fact that's gotten her listed in the *Encyclopedia Yiddishanica* for being Jewish. By the time she was four, her parents divorced.

From the age of five till she was eight she was put in a private school. "They didn't beat me. Just slapped me once. It was just a miserable place. And I don't think any child could really be happy between five and eight away from their parents, do you? No, I don't think so . . . they took away my dolls at night. Why? It was a very confining atmosphere, not a particularly happy time."

Was she considered a "pretty child"? She laughs, thinks for a moment, and says, "I don't know about that. I really don't know. I think I was OK. I was OK. My stepmother once said I was homely, and teased me. I don't think I was ravishing, but I think I was pretty."

Her mother Peggy married wealthy Dr. John Myers, a well-known society figure. Now Tina Myers, she suddenly had the best of everything and graduated from the Scarborough High School in Westchester. There she invented "Louise" for a middle name (society girls were expected to have names a mile long). Of "Tina Louise" she once remarked, "It's entirely my name. To me it means joy. Nobody in any family can be hurt if anything happens to this name because it's my name only."

Tina studied at the Actors Studio. "I was there the same time Joanne Woodward was. . . . Nobody mentions it about me, though." Though she always aspired to be a serious actress, she found her beauty could get her publicity. The Sunday *Mirror* called her "New York Society's No. 1 Debutante." A year later, in 1954, Tina got a full page in the *American Weekly*, headlined MILLIONAIRE CHORUS GIRL. Photos showed her breakfasting in bed, lounging about her "swank apartment," and going out on the town.

Being a chorus girl was at least a show-biz beginning. She appeared in Bette Davis's *Two's Company*, and *Almanac* with Orson Bean. Bean remembers Tina's life-style of the rich and famous—the time she and another chorus girl had a catfight outside the dressing room of the leading man, over who would get inside. "It was like a scene from a movie!" The Sunday *Mirror* reported deb/starlet Tina "went nightclubbing, and very seldom with the same man twice" during a six-month binge. "I had a great time since I was seventeen," she admits now, "a great time."

Well, there were some sour notes. When she spurned one preppie, he punched her in the face—leading to her first newspaper scandal. Tina pressed charges, but the judge shook his head and said, "I understand the feeling of this young man when he saw this beautiful girl with another Romeo." He told the kid to keep away from Tina and let the rest of society's 400 get a chance.

The November 1956 *Pageant* ran a sultry set of photos of Tina in bed in a lace negligee. "She says she's a debutante," a caption said, "but she really wants you to think of her as an actress." It was pictures like these, splattered all over the tabloids, that led Lenny Bruce to mention his lust for those "Tina Louise hooker poses." In 1957 she became Apassionata Von Climax in *Li'l Abner*, sharing a dressing room with Julie Newmar.

"I thought it was great fun at the time," she says, admitting that for her ultimate goal of dramatic parts, other routes might have been taken. Still, it was hard to turn down being a famous cover girl. From 1954 to 1957 the most serious question she got was about her measurements. The Sunday *Mirror* guessed 36-24-37, The Sunday *News* insisted 38-25-38, and the *New York Post* had it 39-24-36—adding that she was five foot eight and a half, 135 pounds, and wore a size-ten shoe.

During *Li'l Abner* Tina was again in a newspaper scandal. It was the divorce battle between her mother and socially prominent Dr. Myers. To spice up the case, the papers ran shots of Tina. Mrs. Myers complained her sixty-seven-year-old husband was a two-timer who held nude "painting classes" with a mistress, and that he refused sex at home, once complaining "I'm writing a book on the fifth dimension. I want to be alone." Another time he said, "Don't bother me. I ate too much for dinner."

The defense claimed forty-three-year-old Mrs. Myers was the one who had strayed. The elderly judge sided with the doctor, insisting "Plaintiff had a most social and luxurious life . . . fine homes, much travel and resplendent clothes and jewelry. It is regrettable that she was unable to steer the marital ship into calm waters . . . every wise woman buildeth her house, but the foolish plucketh it down with her hands."

Tina defended her mother to reporters: "All these things they've been saying are a pack of lies!" After such incidents, it's not surprising that Tina has guarded her own privacy ever since. Questions about her private life are off limits, even relatively mild questions, such as what qualities she looks for in a potential husband.

When the trial ended she was happy. When *Li'l Abner* ended after over six hundred performances, she was even happier. "Believe me, I gave my greatest performances when I knew I was going to leave."

Determined to ditch the sexpot image of the play, she stressed her intellectual side to reporters. They still only saw the backside. James Bacon headlined one story: TINA LOUISE (WHEWEE!) IS GOING INTELLECTUAL. He couldn't understand Tina reading books by Aristotle and Voltaire. He likened it to Marilyn Monroe trading Joe DiMaggio for Arthur Miller. He wrote, "It would take a psychiatrist to explore the hidden relationship between sex appeal and a thirst for knowledge, but it happens."

Tina told Earl Wilson, "I like guys who verbalize more than guys who physicalize. Men imagine that this Don Juan approach appeals to women, but I really think the route to seduction today is by verbalization rather than physicalization."

Said Wilson, "You sound like Amos 'n' Andy."

Tina said, "It's a surer way to a woman's heart to be interested in what she's thinking than what she's wearing or not wearing. For example, how she feels about the coming elections or about planetary problems. You can get tired to the point of tears with this dull, monotonous talk from men about how attractive you are."

She expounded theories of "mental communication without verbalization . . . all space is made up of waves and we are constantly sending and receiving messages from our brain . . . do you understand?" She also talked about politics, declaring her support for Adlai Stevenson in 1960. The joke was not Stevenson running again, but Tina interested in politics.

The *Journal-American* thought it was kooky that she worked out with barbells. "I'm a new woman since I discovered exercise," she said. "I concentrate on exercises from the waist down, since that is the laziest part of a woman's body."

In the '80s a Jane Fonda could get away with being attractive, physically fit, intelligent, and slightly eccentric in her pursuit of new challenges. In the '50s, Tina was seen, but not believed.

Tina doesn't recall herself as necessarily victimized by the panting press, à la Marilyn Monroe. In fact, she didn't think Monroe was victimized either: "She was not a weak person, she was a very strong, serious person." Tina was impressed that Marilyn was able to steer her career well enough to make quality films.

Tina started off her career the same way, winning good notices for her first film, *God's Little Acre* in 1958. She told Joe Hyams that there was more to her role of Griselda than one might imagine: "Griselda only seems sexy because she looks sexy and maybe feels that way but . . . hers is a tragic story and one I know too well. Men just can't keep their hands

off Griselda, because that's the way she affects them. Every time a man sees her he tries to kiss her and rough her up. . . . Sex is a part of her, but is really not her. I understand this so well, because I don't like men to treat me as I look either . . . you don't understand, do you? I'm not one-dimensional at all. If anybody spends any time with me, they learn that. Man, it's rough trying to convince people that I'm really a serious actress."

She was more serious about her career than anything else: "It's the one thing I don't think will ever let me down." Today *God's Little Acre* is still one of Tina's favorite film roles.

She turned down the movie version of *Li'l Abner*, to stay with dramas, and said no to Cary Grant's *Operation Petticoat*. "It went on to make millions of dollars, but I turned it down because it was just a lot of sex jokes."

She entered the '60s fulfilling her plan, appearing in creditable films like *The Hangman* with Robert Taylor, *Day of the Outlaw* with Robert Ryan, and *The Trap* with Richard Widmark. She told reporters to forget her early days "when I was known as a glamour girl . . . it helps an actress get attention when she's starting out," but those days were over.

Her return to Broadway in *Fade Out, Fade In* with Carol Burnett proved she was on her way to a varied career in good shows and movies. Then came *Gilligan's Island*. She left the Broadway show after just a month—promised a starring role on TV by CBS's president and the rest.

"Oh yeah, they kind of sold it to me

that way," she says with a light laugh that sounds less than happy.

Once the show started filming, she was disappointed. So were the critics.

When a *TV Guide* writer visited the set, Tina moaned, "I was ashamed when I saw the first show . . . the show is like a cartoon. You're not acting, not the way I studied it. I wouldn't watch it if I wasn't on it . . . I don't feel fulfilled doing these shows. Most are not quite inventive."

The writer immediately told producer Sherwood Schwartz. "I dare say Miss Louise will always feel unfulfilled," he began. "She's an integral part of a major

♥ In *Warrior Empress* Tina plays a torrid temptress.

hit. What else does an actress want? I don't know what would make her happy. It seems to me that she's not a very happy person. I don't thoroughly understand her."

Some cast members also didn't understand her need for artistic fulfillment, nor did they appreciate the fact that she was definitely the "star" in the eyes of the press. For example, when *TV Guide* ran a cover story on Alan Hale, the cover picture was of . . . Tina Louise. Alan Hale and Bob Denver were out of focus in the background.

Through ninety-eight episodes Tina

♥ Tina, still tops today.

swiveled her way through her sexy, shimmering movie-star costumes, always wearing fresh makeup (the lipstick was supposedly made from raspberries by the thoughtful Professor). As Ginger Grant, the purring, slinky movie queen (sanitized for sitcom TV but still an awe-inspiring sight) Tina was the first "vamp" that '60s boys and girls got to know, the TV version of Marilyn Monroe, putting on the "put-on" role of sexpot the way Marilyn did in her silly sitcom movie *The Seven Year Itch.*

"I was a great fan of hers," Tina admits. "I knew the quality she had, and how to play it so it would work. Originally they had wanted me to play Ginger in a kind of bitchy way, and I really refused. In fact I was ready to quit my job, because I had been asked if I could play a Marilyn Monroe–Lucille Ball type character and I'd said yes. I knew that I was right and [CBS president] James Aubrey agreed with me, and he fired the director."

Eventually there was peace. Says Dawn Wells, "There were some problems initially with Tina a little, but that was all kind of worked out within the first year. It really was family."

Viewers wondering which islanders might "start a family" together figured the only suitable male for Ginger was the Professor. Does Tina agree?

"Oh sure! Oh sure! Absolutely. Absolutely. All beautiful women like intelligent, usually charismatic men." Okay, the Professor wasn't charismatic, but he was nice. "Had he

launched us into space and got us off that island, that would have been charisma," Tina giggles.

The Professor, she admits, had little to do on the show. Actually, Ginger had even less to do. Like Marilyn in *Seven Year Itch*, Tina mostly went through the (sexy) motions. Gilligan and the Skipper did the pratfalls. The Howells were eccentrics. Mary Ann and the Professor were average folk viewers identified with. But Ginger was only there to gawk at. Her natural red hair flamed, her exotic blue eyes glittered with touches of green in just

♥ **Tina bears up beautifully in the midst of *Gilligan's Island* gaggery.**

the right light. Boys and girls got the idea that this was what glamour was all about—what an attractive woman should look and act like.

Tina doesn't care to analyze it. "I think most women like to dress up," she begins. "They probably don't have an opportunity to dress up as often as they would like to. It's sort of fun to dress up for a party. I guess it's a good fantasy show for a lot of people."

Then her voice trails off. "Is that all you're gonna talk about—this dumb show?" She giggles as she says it, but it's plain that being pleasant about the show is straining her patience.

Ginger Grant might glare and walk out the door, a furious prima donna. But Tina Louise explains, with the kind of cheerful voice stewardesses use in discussing oxygen masks, "I don't really want to talk about it anymore. It's boring me! I'm so into *today*, and what's happening *now!* That's so old hat, and to think it's being perpetrated and being put out there again is so boring.

"I don't have anything against it," she begins. "I mean, I'm proud of the success of it." She pauses. "I think it's very charming." She stops: "Amusing. But I certainly don't want to talk too much about it. It's something I did so long ago."

That she still gets fan letters about the show every week seems, at best, a left-handed compliment. The letters are nice, and she adds that she and Bob Denver "were the most outstanding characters that the audience identified with," but it's obvious that a fan identifying her with

Gilligan's is only slightly less embarrassing than being identified in a police lineup.

The show ended up a typecasting nightmare. Barbara Feldon as Agent 99 and Julie Newmar as Rhoda the Robot also played their parts fairly straight, just slightly tongue-in-cheek, but everyone knew Barbara wasn't really a spy, and Julie wasn't really a robot . . . but Tina *was* a movie star. Her identification with Ginger stuck.

After the show was canceled, Tina tried to bury its memory. In the 1969 *Players Guide* (an industry casting directory) Tina didn't even list the show as a credit. Under TV appearances were *Bonanza* and *It Takes a Thief.*

To this day, she doesn't have a single episode of the show on videotape at home. "I certainly don't! I don't have a one. I was the happiest person in the world when that show ended! I was just thrilled—I did not wish to do that show anymore. I didn't want to do it because I wanted to get on to other things.

"I guess I turned down a lot of comedy for about ten years, I wouldn't really touch it after the series. I did one movie of the week, *The Day the Women Got Even*, that was very charming, but I really stayed away from comedy."

She costarred with Dean Martin in *The Wrecking Crew*, then made *The Happy Ending* and *The Good Guys and the Bad Guys*. She ended 1969 filming *How to Commit Marriage*, but wasn't an expert on the subject. Her marriage to Les Crane was brief; they separated in 1970, just

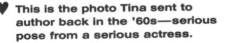

♥ **This is the photo Tina sent to author back in the '60s—serious pose from a serious actress.**

before the birth of their daughter, Caprice.

Starting the '70s caring for the young girl, Tina told a reporter, "I wouldn't say she has replaced my husband, but I've found that my love for my daughter is the most total love you can experience in your life . . . I'm happy to wake up every morning and be with this wonderful little person." She made most of her money doing TV commercials, "a lot more money in one day than in a TV series."

Through the late '70s and early '80s, she concentrated on films like *The Stepford Wives*, *Mean Dog Blues*, and *Night-*

mare in Badham County, a TV film about a women's prison. She learned about real issues in the prison system: "The women in there were not allowed to use their time to learn—to learn accounting, or how to operate a computer. Men were being rehabilitated and given useful things to do, but not the women. I read in *The New York Times* this morning about a woman who has been trying to rise in the hierarchy of a bank. She couldn't break through. You know, a lot of life is controlled by men, and I think there should be more women everywhere, in politics, banks, everywhere a woman wants to go. Little by little, it's happening, by the noise that's being made."

Into the '80s Tina made the TV movie *Friendships, Secrets and Lies* (1979), which remains one of her favorites. At the time, she was fighting against the ghost of Ginger Grant. Not only was *Gilligan's Island* a rerun perennial, the entire cast kept reuniting for TV movies like 1981's *The Harlem Globetrotters on Gilligan's Island*. Tina wasn't about to shipwreck her career further. At the time Bob Denver said, "I don't know how she can think one two-hour movie can tarnish her image, when *Gilligan* is showing five times a day everywhere in the country." Today Dawn Wells says, "We understood her and knew where she was coming from. We weren't surprised that she didn't do the movies."

Some years were tough. There are films Tina wishes she hadn't made, like *Evils of the Night*. It was "terrible. That should have been called *Had to Work*. I mean you people out there don't seem to realize that actors have families to support. It's a business, it's not like you do what you want every single second! There's only so much work out there."

Tina starred in the soap opera *Rituals*, and appeared on *Dallas, Blacke's Magic, Simon & Simon,* and *Knight Rider.* Fans saw that no matter what the script, Tina was still worth watching, as glamorous and intriguing as ever.

She keeps herself in shape with an exercise regimen. "I like to create energy, I like to work out early in the day and begin creating that energy. I work out for an hour to the Jane Fonda tape at home. I'm not an outside girl, I'm an inside girl. Staying out of the sun is mandatory! With my exercises, I work out at my own speed, I'll press the pause button now and then—but I *get through it!* Exercise is very important. So is sleep—you've got to get enough sleep. Also, you have to take care of your skin."

After her morning exercises, and a fast shower, Tina treats her skin to its own exercises that open and tighten the pores. She fills the sink with ice cubes and water, and lets the faucet in the tub run hot. "I splash my face with the ice water, and alternate with hot water from the bathtub. It's very good for waking up the skin. I do it seventy times. Heat contracts the skin. It's great if there's any swelling around the eyes." A light application of facial cream helps too.

"Of course what you put into your body is as important. You should eat the right foods. What you think—oh that's very

important—what you think! I believe in the power of the mind." Tina doesn't necessarily mean anything occult—just common sense. "For instance if you have a negative thought, a lot of people will spend hours thinking about it when it's really so simple to put in a positive and immediately direct the mind to positive energy. I feel really strongly about that. Your day is very much affected by what you allow yourself to digest mentally. If somebody says something bad to you, how long are you going to think about it? A week? Three months? A year? My theory is you're not going to think about it at all; put in another thought and repeat that thought over until you're not thinking of the negative thought."

Nineteen eighty-seven's movie *After All These Years* is something she can dismiss that easily: "Yeah. Yeah. There's nothing in that. They botched that up."

Some sexy stars like Raquel Welch and Farrah Fawcett have earned dramatic praise by taking unflattering roles. Tina doesn't believe she must forsake glamour to be taken seriously: "I can look as plain as anybody! It's very very easy to look plain! An actress can look any way she wants to. But I think it's fun to wear beautiful clothes and to be attractive—*and* to be emotional. You know, like the early Katharine Hepburn films. She's my idol. I just love her."

Tina is hoping to star in a series of "contemporary dramas, stories about the relationship between the sexes, the interaction between men and women." Asked if she would've liked a glamorous/

dangerous role like Glenn Close's part in *Fatal Attraction*, she says, "I won't mention a role that's already been done. I'm too original for that. I want to create my own. The film that I just did is very original. It's *The Pool,* directed by Luis Aira. It's quite glamorous and it's also very emotional, the perfect vehicle for me. I like to do feature films because I don't like being locked up in a series. I don't like to work every day—it's not my personality, I don't like to have to do something the same every single day."

Every single day, a certain silly sitcom is rerun. Many fans still watch the show for some fun nostalgia. But if Ginger Grant is frozen in time, Tina Louise is not. The fascination with Tina Louise is still there, a mature actress ready to make mature films for mature fans. She could be making some fascinating films in the near future.

♥ The sexy starlet as a teasing "Eve."

Julie Newmar

MY LIVING DOLL

First broadcast: September 27, 1964
Last broadcast: September 8, 1965

BATMAN

First broadcast: January 12, 1966
Last broadcast: March 14, 1968

If ever the term *goddess* applied to an actress, it's to five-foot-ten, 145-pound, 38-23-38, 135-IQ Julie Newmar. She even seems to have the life-span of a goddess, her beauty unchanged in three decades.

The awesome perfection people perceive in Julie has come with a price. Julie's "unbelievable" presence has meant being typecast in supernatural, superhuman roles. As a '60s sweetheart, she played "the perfect woman" (Rhoda the robot) and the "purrr-fect" villainess (Catwoman).

Born—not created in a lab—on August 16, 1935, in Los Angeles, Julia Charlene Newmeyer's mother was redheaded Helen Jesmer, star of the *Follies* of 1920. Her father, six-foot-four Donald Newmeyer, was a professor at Los Angeles State.

Julie, the child of this perfect match, was not perfect in childhood: "I was introverted, shy, and withdrawn. I suffered. My first emotion about myself was that I was unattractive. My father told me I wasn't pretty. I had thin legs and big feet." Even during her fame as *My Living Doll* she told *TV Guide* that most performers "are the unloved—that's why

119

we make such a spectacle of ourselves."

Ballet helped her feel more graceful. She also took piano lessons, getting up at six A.M. to practice. She studied Christian Science, "an enormously positive influence in my life. I remember Sunday school with a great deal of positive passion and warmth and support. It gave me a lot of clarity in my life, it eased my life, I didn't struggle with a lot of negative emotion. Do you know what I mean? I would walk onstage just aglow, a positive feeling of how great and good a place it was to be. Christian Science gives you that positive power."

Julie's own ideal of perfection was Rita Hayworth. "Of course there's a physical similarity, color of hair, height. I even studied dance from not only her father but her uncle. I tried to grow my nails like her, etc., etc. I still do my makeup and hair like her."

An excellent student who had a pinup picture of Albert Einstein in her room, Julie graduated from John Marshall High when she was fifteen, and was already a prima ballerina for the Los Angeles Opera. She left UCLA to be both choreographer and dancer in films like *Demetrius and the Gladiators*, *East of Sumatra*, *Serpent of the Nile*, and *Slaves of Babylon*. The first role she considers at all memorable was in *Seven Brides for Seven Brothers*. She used her money to come to New York and try out for Broadway musicals.

In 1955 she made her Broadway debut as the ballerina in *Silk Stockings*. Things happened quickly after that. There was a quick romance with author Louis

L'Amour, and quick fame for her ninety-second role as Stupefyin' Jones in *Li'l Abner*. This was the first of Julie's many supernatural roles, a Medusa in reverse, a woman so beautiful she turned men to stone. What really stupefied the press was that she was as bright as she was beautiful. In this Monroe-Mansfield era when ditsy sex kitten talk was expected, Julie talked about religion, classical piano, and ballet.

"It's no achievement to be beautiful," she told the press. "It was an inheritance from my mother. I won a number of Miss-Something-Or-Other contests, stupid things like 'Miss Maple Syrup.' It's what else you have that's important."

Still, boggled columnists like Sidney Skolsky actually printed *all* her measurements ("Her ankles are 7½ inches, her calf 13½ and her thighs 21 inches in circumference"), stared at her long (38 inches) legs, and asked what kind of mortal man had the best chance with her. She said, "I intend to marry a rich, handsome genius, probably a writer."

Magazines printed the big pictures— and whatever titillating tidbits columnists could find (or make up). Yes, she dated short men too: "They have a great deal more drive than other men. They are aggressive—they have to be because of their size." Yes, she slept in a giant bed—"Four people could get into it and not see each other." Yes, she slept nude: "If I ever wear anything, it will surely have lace on it. I must feel pretty in bed." No, she didn't like wearing lipstick: "I might want to kiss someone." Yes, she

♥ **Stupefyin': Julie literally stopped the show when she made her Broadway debut in *Li'l Abner*.**

enjoyed nude swimming: "Such freedom, such exhilaration!" And why did she think men were so fascinated with her goddesslike height? "All men have a touch of adventure in them: when they see a mountain they want to conquer it."

She sometimes gave answers that befitted a goddess. She told *The New York Times*, "I want the best of everything . . . the best fruit, the best clothes, the best underwear, even if I'm the only one who knows I'm wearing it."

Her next Broadway role was in *The Marriage-Go-Round*. At last allowed to speak, she demonstrated a natural gift for comic timing. As the sexy Swede who nearly breaks up Charles Boyer's marriage, she won a Tony award for Best Supporting Actress. Today the lusty, busty Swedish girl is a cliché, but at the time she virtually originated the concept, and played it to the hilt—for laughs.

The highlight scene had Julie strut into the professor's den wearing nothing but a towel. She wore nothing underneath. As she told Earl Wilson at the time, "It says in the script that she comes in from a sunbath perfectly nude and throws a towel around her. So I said, 'We've got to be realistic. Remember Stanislavsky!' I hold it up with—well, I don't breathe. I hold it up with one finger, if anything. There was one man in Philadelphia who came several nights. His wife told me, 'He's certain one night that towel's going to fall off.'"

Julie wasn't really kidding about Stanislavsky—she was schooled at the Actors Studio. As Katrin in the play, she developed a new facet of her persona: "Scandinavian cool on the outside and let them guess what's broiling inside." The only real drawback was dying her hair blond: "I didn't like it, because when I looked in the mirror I thought I looked like an insipid, angelic type. With my natural hair, I look evil. That I like. It's not that I'm really evil, I just like to look evil is all."

She was called "out of this world," "awe-inspiring" and "amazing," both for

♥ Julie won a Tony for her role as a sexy Swede in *Marriage-Go-Round.*

her mind and body, but this wasn't what Julie particularly wanted. She explained to *The New York Times,* "Tell me I'm beautiful, it's nothing. Tell me I'm intellectual—I know it. Tell me I'm funny and it's the greatest compliment in the world anyone could give me."

The secret of Julie's appeal is just that: a sense of fun that puts the perfection of mind and body just slightly askew. Perfection is boring—Julie is not. Within an hour of casual conversation she'll giggle like a girl, laugh like a wicked catwoman, whisper passionately in making a point, begin a sentence with deep philosophical

and intellectual intent, and end it with a poker-faced aside brimming with humor. Call her unpredictable—or just a lot of fun.

Some degree of her heat, coolness, and comedy was captured on Broadway. But as the '60s turned, she was still looking for the right vehicle to put it all together. After the national tour of *Stop the World I Want to Get Off* and some blond movie roles (from *The Rookie* to *For Love or Money*) she played a blond devil, complete with horns, dangerously fulfilling a man's wish in a *Twilight Zone* episode that aired in April 1963.

From a devil, she became a doll— the beautiful brunette Rhoda the robot on *My Living Doll.* She was well cast for it. In some poses she resembled a porcelain doll: the round forehead, prominent high cheekbones, and hint of dimples. She could press her lips together in a very enigmatic pout—a doll's mouth that could be kissed, but did not necessarily promise to kiss back.

My Living Doll was tinkered together by producer Jack Chertok, creator of *My Favorite Martian* the year before. Julie's style was to blend sophistication and naïveté alluringly; natural heat encased in unnatural cool. Sadly, sitcoms of the day were not on her level. The sophisticated theme of man's passion for the perfect (and perfectly controllable) woman turned to formula mush when sitcom veteran Bob Cummings was called in to star as Dr. Bob McDonald. About as witty as the script got was having her control buttons be beauty marks on her back.

It wasn't a total loss; Julie's sense of fantasy fun and her unique combination of intelligence and imagination showed through the tired scripts. She was funny as the misunderstanding Robot AF709 that took commands literally, suffered mechanical failures that left her acting drunk or dizzy, yet remained unperturbed by the chaos around her. (No wonder Dr. Bob explained to friends that his lady friend was really a "psychiatric patient" under his care!)

As a "living doll," Julie recalls, about eighty percent of her fan mail was from males. The girls who did write in were the tall ones—writing in to find out how to achieve such grace and perfection. Julie made it look easy. Yet, Jayne Mansfield made naïveté seem crass. Mamie Van Doren made sensuality cheap. Anita Ekberg made Swedish perfection spooky. Jane Fonda made intelligence obnoxious. Julie put it all together with grace.

At the time, sci-fi writer Isaac Asimov noted that Rhoda was "a poorly designed robot who must receive very careful treatment and very sensitive handling if she is to flourish." Rhoda received poor treatment. Cummings wasn't the right costar and Sunday night at 9 P.M. opposite *Bonanza* was the wrong time slot. In one year, the robot was switched off.

It took a few years, but Julie's next supernatural role would be her biggest hit. "I have yet to have the perfect explanation of why that show was so successful for me," Julie says today. She still gets tons of fan mail from people trying to express

their delight with her performance as Catwoman on *Batman*. She reads from one recent letter: "You've always been my favorite villainess and you'll never know how much I long to be one of your goons. You were always so nice for someone who was supposed to be evil . . ."

Julie doesn't have tapes of her *My Living Doll* or *Batman* episodes. She has no Catwoman paraphernalia around the house. "No need to. I'm reminded of it every day when I go out! Sometimes it's just the gleam in the eye of a boy or now a man who says 'You brought me through puberty!'"

♥ **Autographed photo sent to the author at the time of *My Living Doll*.**

She laughs. "Wow! I get that positive sexual identification. Not a whorey or a negative one. It pleases me deeply that it's positive. And pure in a sense. You are as long as you're up on the screen and not handled."

Julie's appeal, befitting a "goddess," does have that "no-touch" element. Her beauty is classic—more awe-inspiring than explicitly arousing. Isn't it true that fans tend to view her as an ideal—the epitome of beauty, talent, and intelligence? "Yes, that's it, you put your finger on it there," Julie agrees, more out of a musing sense of wonder than ego. All this talk of perfection and awesome beauty baffles her.

"That's what I am, there's no big deal. You thank your parents for your genes, the fact that your mother told you not to take sun baths. Simple things like that. Some think I might've had a facelift, which I've not! To me, I'm not special. I don't even like the concept of special, that someone is more special than another. To me all human souls are equal, and that includes the most handicapped person. I'm not above them."

Amateur psychologists might note that Batman himself was in awe of her. There was no question that Catwoman was his complete equal, and that every smirk and purr unnerved him. Perhaps young fans, with good reason both to want and fear a larger-than-life symbol of female perfection, identified with Batman's delightful plight.

Catwoman's teasing of Batman was much more exciting than the occasional quasi-love scenes. "I wasn't so fond of that mushy stuff," she says, laughing. "I felt that as the villain you made yourself too vulnerable . . . so I would look down on sipping sodas with Batman!"

Another important part of Catwoman was the voice. At last, Julie's unique and expressive voice was used as a key to her character. It can register gently lilting calm one minute, passionate intensity the next. She could be as gleeful as a child when taunting Batman; cool and intellectual when plotting a crime; and dryly humorous in both triumph and defeat.

As Catwoman, the sheer fun Julie was having with the role made her a villain people didn't love to hate—they just loved her. Probably the only other villain on *Batman* with whom fans had as much fun was Vincent Price, one of the few masters of the same kind of magical "naughty good time" that Julie purveyed.

Julie debuted as Catwoman on March 16, 1966. She would only play the role in five two-part episodes, but it was more than enough time to make her the show's favorite villainess; a TV immortal. Her debut episode was even made into a View Master slide presentation.

Her only regret is that the filming was always rushed. The payment wasn't much either: $1,250 and no rerun royalties.

Julie's career jump-started all over again after her success on *Batman*. She turned up as Mother Nature—on a Dutch Masters cigar commercial, first aired January 22, 1967. She played a bizarre beauty who could turn into a kind of werewolf-Afghan in the forgettable *Mal-*

tese Bippy. She was a psychotic Indian with a gorgeous body and scarred face in *Mackenna's Gold*. Neither film was a hit; the latter was a severe disappointment—an all-star cast brought down by a boring script and somnolent direction. Even Julie's gratuitous nude scene was more farcical than sensual as she battled Camilla Sparv and Gregory Peck under water.

Playboy acquired some on-the-set shots and published them. Not pleased, but not that upset, she wrote to this author, in May 1968, "Thank you for your letter, support, and whatever admiration since the printing of the *Playboy* article . . . but I didn't 'pose' for *Playboy*. As a matter of fact the set was absolutely closed to all photographers and visitors. The none-too-clear photographs were taken by the Wardrobe Department . . . Frankly, I don't care one way or the other about nudity or non-nudity. Morality is how you behave toward people. What people want to think of me, or anyone else, is their problem. They live with it, not me. Best wishes and continued success and I hope happiness . . ."

Since Julie was busy with *Mackenna's Gold*, Eartha Kitt played Catwoman in the last episodes. But, as Alan Napier (Alfred on the show) says, "Julie Newmar was the best Catwoman"—the one and only Cat-woman.

Julie made appearances on other TV shows, including *The Monkees* and *Star Trek*. Into the '70s Julie costarred in several TV movies. In *The Feminist and the Fuzz* she played a hooker, a role she played quite often, the casting logic evidently being that the average mortal could get this larger-than-life beauty only for a price. She also played a variety of eccentrics *(A Very Missing Person, Terraces)*. "I always get a little put off when people say 'kooky,' and yet they're right," Julie admits. "I think that's because I've never been on the inside. I'm a person who's an outsider. Not desiring to get in, by the way."

She toured the country in stage productions of *Damn Yankees, Dames at Sea*, and even *The Marriage-Go-Round*, this time deciding to add a naughty few seconds of real nudity to her towel scene. In 1977 Julie turned up in *People* almost nude—demurely turning her back to the camera, wearing nothing but high heels and revealing pantyhose. She was promoting her invention, "Nudemar" pantyhose that could turn a woman's derriere into a round "apple instead of a ham sandwich" thanks to an elastic back seam separating the cheeks. She didn't need them ("being a ballet dancer, I'm very firm"), but was hoping to uplift millions of women around the nation. She got patent number 4,003,094, but is still waiting for backers to help lift the backsides. "Pantyhose flatten you out and in doing so also make you look flatter and lower. I suppose that's why women have not demanded [her uplifting invention]—they don't see themselves in the back!"

That year Julie met a Texas oil man named John Smith at a party. They married in August and she went home with him: "Oh, I thought I was going to retire!

Retire! My dear, I moved to Fort Worth, Texas!" She pauses. "I was an outsider. No one would talk to me there. I didn't have any friends there . . . they thought I was some weird thing from outer space."

Her despair didn't last too long. "My child was born when I was forty-eight," says Julie. "God you appreciate the child so much, it's so incredible, it's not something that came along too early—fabulous, every moment with him is a treasure. It's totally changed my life."

When the marriage fell apart, Julie made a quick return to films (*Evils of the Night*, a low point for her as well as for costar Tina Louise and probably even for Aldo Ray and John Carradine). Then she found something better: the real estate business. "My mother owned some rather dilapidated property and reluctantly— very reluctantly—gave me the managership of it. But I had no support from my husband who had sort of disappeared, left home let's say, and I needed to support my son and I wanted to be home, not in some movie studio sixteen hours a day. So I created this job, you see. But it took a lot of studying and at night I would go to UCLA and take real estate courses, and I could barely understand what they were saying about finance, they were very sophisticated classes. I struggled through it, but I'm not in fear anymore about money, which was kind of a bête noire in my family—it was in the old sense like

♥ **Julie was purrfect as Catwoman.**

sex, you didn't talk about it. But these days you not only have to talk about it, you have to handle it. You could see how masculine money was. [Whispers.] You can't touch it! It's not yours. It becomes like a phallus!"

Julie vowed not to make any more exploitation films from writers and directors in "cocaine alley." With a multimillion-dollar real estate business, she can choose her roles with care. She can stay home and be with her young son.

Much of her success, inner calm, and tranquillity has come from her religious philosophies. Not completely a Christian Scientist (she took her son to the hospital when he had meningitis) her blend of "thought philosophies" has created something unique and personal. "But everything is a point of view. No religion should be the only religion in this world. It simply turns my stomach when I hear these video preachers say 'You gonna die if you don't support Christ!' Yes, but . . . it looks like *you're* the one that's gonna kill me! But everyone is right in his own way—that to me is very important. Everyone's right coming from their own experience, you see. I try to keep an emotional calm. Christian Science is just a genius of a discovery. *Genius!* The greatest thing that Christians have to offer *is* forgiveness, that's probably the greatest thing that Christ came on this earth to deliver to us. Now my brother's an atheist— or an agnostic, I'm not sure—oh well, he has such a nice surprise coming!"

Julie doesn't proselytize, to her brother or anyone else. "No, someone must come to you with great desire to know, or to share, and people don't. . . . There must be faith. And when you're in the depth of pain, it's something that you have. And then finally it becomes a reality, your faith, your belief. Struggle is wonderful. Failure is fabulous. Poverty is the greatest wealth-maker of all."

Like many '60s sweethearts, Julie is upset with the changes in values that have come in the '80s (and which have sparked renewed interest in the morality of the '60s). "What's the important word in what you said? Value. We've been very—not demoralized—but there's a moral sinking. I think that Vietnam brutalized us. When I look at what I see in much younger people, I don't see enough good manners, an idea of any moral restraint. It's a kind of chaos. Freedom is expensive." The '60s "was an age of romance. It's so depressing now to see kids with drugs, how much they're depriving themselves of genuinely finding out and experiencing something."

Julie's high energy level may be part of the reason she remains so youthful. Her health secrets are only slightly "mystical." She believes that a healthy mind produces a healthy body, but she also follows some down-to-earth techniques. "I take a ballet class at least three times a week. It's so hard, it's just killing, but it's really beautifying." Don't mention aerobics. "Uch," she says. "Disgusting. All those people frumping around, their minds numbed by that noise. That does damage to your inner sensitivity, your inner system, and think of the damage it does to your body. Thumping! You're not a horse! One should move gracefully; swimming, dance, tennis—a movement that beautifies one within and without." Julie believes in hard work, but not pain. "It must feel right. I've never ever hurt myself. Not even a strained muscle. Never hurt yourself! Love yourself! You're the universe from which you see other universes, other people out there."

Julie takes vitamins "for insurance," including a powdered mix of liver powder and spirulina in tomato juice. "It immediately brings my strength up. I'm not cranky. I immediately feel stronger and more pacific. It's absolutely awful," she laughs. "I wouldn't recommend it to anybody."

Julie's one diet regimen is eating the same thing every morning—fruit and cottage cheese. "I love butter and ice cream and things like that, but I wouldn't pig out. It's more like an ecstasy treat. The point is if something might make you fat you better enjoy every tiny mouthful of it! Take very small bites and then it's OK. People will tell me they love to watch me eat because I have this ecstatic way of chewing the 'no-no' foods to make them last."

A robot, a catwoman, various prostitutes—after all these years, Julie realizes she'll never play "normal" roles. She doesn't want to. She wants to try a part that accentuates her supernatural attributes, but rather than adding Catwoman evil, draws from her own personality, so influenced by Christian Science, Krishnamurti, and helping others.

♥ **Still a formidable fantasy figure in the '80s.**

"I have this dream," she begins in a confidential whisper. "Since I'm very successful with characters that are larger than life, I want to be almost a semigod-dess who has come to earth. She has this knowledge of how it's like to be on this earth in perfect harmony. I'd like to see a lot of magic in this character, like *Star Wars* without the war. I'll be able to fly, or go around the universe with my thoughts, the camera and you being able to see what I can see with my heart and my consciousness."

When will this project fly? "This may take time, but time doesn't exist, as long as you have it in mind." She pauses. "Your mind had to think up this book—you got to me through your mind—so here I am physically, because you commanded it. This project will happen. After all, we're gonna be able to do this stuff. We *are* going to be able to do this stuff, so why not start bringing it in now?"

Meanwhile, fans are still fascinated by the fantasy figure of Catwoman. Many have complete collections of videos and photos, and love it when Julie makes occasional appearances at comic book conventions and colleges. "It's just befuddling," she purrs. "But I think it's so sweet."

Barbara Eden ❀

I DREAM OF JEANNIE

First broadcast: September 18, 1965
Last broadcast: September 1, 1970

"I wish women were like genies: If you wanted one, you could pop her out of the bottle, then put her back in there afterward."

A quote from male chauvinist supreme, Bobby Riggs. He'd evidently seen *I Dream of Jeannie.*

The show was "total woman" fantasy—for men who wanted a blonde who'd do almost anything to please, and for women who vicariously wanted the thrill of playing harem girl to the era's big male hero symbol, an astronaut. Here was bachelor astronaut Tony Nelson living it up with Jeannie. They weren't even married (at least, not for the first three years of the five-year run). But—this was the '60s. And it was all good, clean fun. Wasn't it?

It was, thanks to Barbara Eden, who played the genie who was born April 1, 64 B.C., but never looked a day over thirty.

Eden was born Barbara Jean Moorhead in Tucson, Arizona, August 23, 1934. When her parents divorced she moved to San Francisco with her mother. Her mother then married Harrison Huffman, a phone lineman, and Barbara took his name. Later, she met a real Barbara Eden. Since that lady wasn't in show business, she simply borrowed the name.

"Barbara was always singing and performing," her mother Alice says. "When she was just sixteen she was in *Spring*

Crazy, a play written by Richard Barthelmess's wife Mary." Barbara's mother even sewed costumes for her daughter.

Barbara tried nightclub singing next, but it wasn't a glamorous life. The shy teen couldn't deal with the all-male bands contemptuous of the "chirp" who was geting all the attention. Once she became so rattled onstage she couldn't perform. The bandleader just muttered, "Don't sing—just smile." After a year studying theater at City College she moved to Hollywood.

Barbara was a real-life pixie, only five feet four inches tall. She had those bright, innocent eyes and those long, thick eyelashes. Her first "biggie" was becoming a semiregular on *The Johnny Carson Show,* the prime-time series Johnny did in 1956. Then she played Loco in 1958's syndicated *How to Marry a Millionaire* sitcom. The show was shot at 20th Century–Fox, along with a Western called *Broken Arrow.* As a publicity gimmick, Barbara met the star of that show, Michael Ansara. It was no gimmick when they married in January of 1958.

They were an interesting contrast—the scowling, balding, serious Ansara and the lighthearted, ebullient Barbara. As she said, "I've always liked authoritative, very masculine, romantic men . . . the big studios are getting away from putty-faced soft-looking guys playing characters with no spines." The Ansaras owned a ranch house in Sherman Oaks, complete with pool. She loved to swim, even in the rain. The couple enjoyed riding their bikes along the winding local roads. If they wanted more sport, they went down to the bowling alley they owned.

As the '60s began, Barbara was the envy of teenage girls everywhere, playing opposite Elvis Presley in *Flaming Star* and Pat Boone in *All Hands on Deck.* Columnists begged her to compare the two. "Elvis," Barbara said at the time, "is very quiet and moody. Pat Boone is the reverse . . . more the extrovert in person. Basically, though, they're both shy and sensitive. They warm up only when they know you and feel a rapport."

An article on Barbara was actually titled "The Girl Who Kissed Pat Boone." Instead of pandering to the publicity, Barbara admitted she was married and explained that giving Pat his very first screen kiss was acting, "not emotional."

She remembers playing "a crazy variety of parts. In *The Seven Faces of Dr. Lao* I was an emotionally dried-up widow. In *The New Interns* I was a fast-talking, curvy, flashy nurse. In *The Confession* I was a pregnant prostitute who hears St. Joseph speak. In *Ride the Wild Surf,* a teenage surfer."

She also costarred in *The Brass Bottle,* about a man (Tony Randall) who finds a genie in a bottle. Burl Ives played the genie. *The New York Times* called Ives "amiable" and "ponderous," but noted that Barbara Eden, the female lead, was "cute and decorative." The movie hasn't aged as well as *Jeannie.* As *The New York*

♥ **Barbara in a typically incongruous starlet pose, oaring around at M-G-M.**

(132)

Times now describes it in their TV listings: "About as funny as your own funeral."

For *Jeannie* the plot was just as simple. Captain (later promoted to Major) Tony Nelson, marooned on an island after a NASA mission, rubs a bottle on the beach and out pops the most beautiful genie in the world. A true sitcom dope, he refuses to take her along with him, but this bottled imp won't be denied. She tags along anyway, ready for more than a hundred episodes of fun and frolic!

The genie she began playing in 1965 was something very special and she knew it. "It's funny," she told the *New York Post*'s Barry Cunningham at the time, "when I was at Fox, I never was treated as a big sex symbol. I was the super-ingenue in films. Always sung to, danced with, carried away. In this series I'm being treated as a woman finally. It's flattering." She described her private life's pleasures as "Simple. I love to be sent flowers and told I'm beautiful."

Barbara was pregnant with her son Matthew just before shooting began on the show. "We had to start shooting early that year so we could take a long break when I couldn't work," she recalls. "Genie costumes are difficult if you are trying to conceal anything."

The genie costume created a furor; NBC censors hadn't seen anything like it. Neither had anyone else. The outfit was actually a Spanish bolero jacket on top, an Oriental dancer's belt hugging her middle, and Arabian pantaloons billowing over her legs. What NBC's censors saw, the rest of the country would not! They forced Barbara to wear lined pantaloons so that her legs wouldn't show. Then they took dead-center aim on Barbara's navel and fired out one word: "No!"

It was the most famous navel battle in TV history. Newspapers jeered the coverup. When Barbara asked the show's producer why her navel was forbidden, "He just stared off into space. I can't find anyone on the show that will give me a logical reason for hiding it. The poor little thing is being discriminated against!"

Sometimes Barbara hid her navel with a wide belt, but often the wardrobe department cheated—sliding her pants down and simply inserting a flesh-colored plug into the offending belly button!

The censors felt the low-slung pants were too suggestive of lounging pajamas—which could be lowered further any minute. After all, here was an unmarried genie parading around the house in very intimate attire! During the run of *Jeannie*, Barbara did get a chance to show her navel—when she starred in *Kismet* on a rival network.

Originally there were lyrics to the *I Dream of Jeannie* theme. The opening stanza: "Jeannie, fresh as a daisy, just look how she obeys me, does things that just amaze me so . . ." They were deleted because they sounded too provocative, or too stupid.

Ironically, the navel incident was not the first time censors looked below Barbara's waistline for controversy. In 1959 she played a Wac in *A Private's Affair* with Gary Crosby. As columnist Herb Stein reported back then: "Barbara wore no girdle. Inasmuch as Miss Eden has a provocative derriere, the Army raised objections to the lack of wraparound, insisted the bundle of joy be properly encased . . ."

Though Eden lost to NBC's censors, designer Bob Mackie believes that the costume was enough—as long as it was Barbara inside it. "What made her work was that she didn't look like what an Arabian genie was supposed to look like. She looked like a blond, busty, bright-eyed, middle-class American girl." Aside from her looks, she also had a distinctive voice; there was joy in it, a childlike sense of delight. Even when angry, she sounded cute.

Though her image was sexy, Barbara is remembered as being a hard worker on the set, devoid of pretension. If anyone was a problem, it was Larry Hagman, who could be a little strange at times. In fact he nearly was bounced from the show for making one demand too many "for the good of the show."

"What makes Jeannie so sexy is that she doesn't play sex," said executive producer Sidney Sheldon. Producer Claudio Guzman added that the magic in *Jeannie* was due to Barbara: "You figure, well, just another pretty girl. Then you look again. Sure, she's got everything. But she ain't shaking it. Then you look at the part. It's insipid. One of those cutesy-pie roles that's nowhere unless you've got the right girl. What she's got can't be faked. It is the real female-animal quality." Guzman told writer Dwight Whitney that one of the

♥ **The serious side of the starlet.**

reasons the show worked so well was that Barbara herself reined in the sexuality of the character. As part of her "basic conservatism," she kept the part squeaky clean.

But, for an interesting twist, Tony Randall, her coworker in *The Brass Bottle*, says, "Barbara is the hippest chick who ever—unintentionally—deluded anyone into thinking she's a goody-goody square. Barbara has a wonderfully bawdy sense of humor that not everyone gets to know."

It was that fascinating mix of sprightly cuteness and sultry earthiness that kept audiences guessing through so many half hours, beginning in that very first episode when (imprisoned in the bottle for not

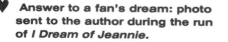

bachelor apartment . . . her 'master' and 'slave' relationship . . . comic as it is, seems better suited to the Marquis de Sade."

Through 139 episodes, the show came to rely on gimmicks (the old "twin sister" trick among others) and endless guest stars, from Paul Lynde, Jerry Quarry, Don Rickles, Richard Loo, and Groucho Marx to Michael Ansara as both Blue Djinn and King Kamehameha and Judy Carne as Jeannie's cousin Myrt. There were minor parts for soon-to-be-stars like Farrah Fawcett. A few new twists were written in along the way—Jeannie let silly Roger Healey (Bill Daily) discover her true identity, but NASA psychiatrist Major Bellows (Hayden Rorke) forever stayed confused.

Fans writing in to Barbara got a portrait of her—but Vietnam soldiers got something special. Husband Michael Ansara told her to send the fighting men a full body shot. He knew what they really wanted to see!

Unfortunately Ansara fans weren't seeing much of him. He wasn't finding enough work to keep himself busy. "I don't think it is right for the wife to leave her husband at home every day," Barbara said, sounding just like the supportive, sympathetic Jeannie. "I know Mike doesn't like it. He wants me home, and he wants to star in a series. We're both trying to find a solution to the problem." It was a problem a playacting genie couldn't solve.

I Dream of Jeannie went off the air in

♥ **Answer to a fan's dream: photo sent to the author during the run of *I Dream of Jeannie*.**

marrying the evil Blue Djinn) she was released by Captain Tony Nelson to utter those immortal words, "Thou may ask anything of thy slave, master."

The show always had a "double standard" to it. Kids loved it and the magical genie who got into silly, sister-vs.-brother type antics. But older viewers wondered—Jeannie was playful in the daytime, but what about the nights? In 1968, *TV Guide* admitted *Jeannie* was "actually one of the most daring shows on TV . . . the only show in which an attractive unmarried girl has the free run of a

1970, the beginning of a decade of heart-breaking changes for Barbara. In 1971 she had a miscarriage in the seventh month of her pregnancy. The child that would have brought the couple closer together now drove them further apart. Barbara threw herself into her career again, performing all over the country. The couple separated, and a year later divorced.

Barbara was torn apart by the divorce, even though she had initiated it. As for Ansara, he could only tell reporters, "I'm confused. I never did any of those things that women can't forgive. I don't drink excessively, gamble, or run around with other girls . . . perhaps she suddenly felt she didn't need me anymore. It is so unbelievably sad. I've been married to Barbara for fifteen years—and I still love her."

Professionally, Barbara had six or seven fairly lean years of low TV exposure, making TV movies like *The Feminist and the Fuzz* and *Guess Who's Sleeping in My Bed.* A 1972 variety special, *Love Is . . . Barbara Eden,* was panned by *Variety* as "uniformly mediocre," thanks to uninteresting songs and skits. "It wasn't a question of not being wanted," Barbara recalls. "The shows they found just didn't work. The parts they found weren't any fun."

In the TV movie *Let's Switch!* she played a housewife married with two kids—who trades places with Barbara Feldon, feminist editor of *She* magazine. Dismally dated now, with its bell-bottoms, alfalfa sprouts, and shouts of

♥ **She grants Major Nelson's every wish—even if it's just for water.**

"Right on," it was padded with mild sitcom humor (Eden accidentally sets off the sprinkler system in a restaurant and Feldon protests a PTA book-burning session—only to discover they're destroying old, falling-apart textbooks). It had a few well-meaning tidbits of '70s wisdom. At the end, Eden convinces her husband that she needs, if not a career, some meaningful self-expression: "There's more to life than washing dishes and changing diapers . . . the kids will grow up and leave and I'll be sitting there in that kitchen."

Barbara tried to balance cuteness and fantasy with the 1974 pilot, *The Barbara Eden Show*, in which she played a toy designer. The networks toyed with it, but didn't buy it.

She was more successful playing in clubs around the country. *Variety* noted in 1974, "Eden has . . . an appealing figure, which her animated presentation of tunes more or less flaunts. Songstress also has a good voice."

Meanwhile *Jeannie* didn't disappear in the '70s after all. She was a hit in reruns. Feminists were dismayed to see *I Dream of Jeannie* still around—and guys still dreaming about a love slave.

Was *Jeannie* the ultimate sexist show? Barbara never bought that. When *TV Guide* asked her about the old show, she explained, "Jeannie wasn't a wimp or a robot. She really had a mind of her own. People in the women's movement would sometimes say, 'How can you call him master?' My own personal little bit of philosophy is that I don't think what we say is as important as what we do. She was saying 'Yes master,' but she was always doing her own thing. Jeannie was certainly an independent woman; she was never a doormat."

When asked about 70s issues, like vasectomy, she had answers: "The vasectomy is all right with me, if a man can handle it. I mean, if it doesn't hurt his manhood. Look, there are people who keep having children, too many children, and there's a time to stop, unless you're of a religious persuasion to just keep going on."

Barbara met Charles Fegert, a vice president with a Chicago newspaper. Fegert looked like Robert Lansing, with graying temples and a square jaw. But he was no actor. "I find that the limelight bothers me," he confided to a reporter. "It scares me. I'm not crazy about publicity and I'm not used to the focus being on me. I can understand that Barbara is newsworthy, but I'm certainly not." He did let his newspaper get exclusive honeymoon pix, including a bubble-bath shot of Barbara, but friends said he was disturbed that he, a very influential figure in Chicago, was upstaged constantly by Barbara's figure.

Barbara and Charles separated in 1980 and divorced in 1982. A few years later, she began to see a lot of Dr. Stanley Frileck, a plastic surgeon. The doctor saw beneath the gorgeous skin: "You look at her, and you think, 'This is a blonde with not much there,'" he told reporter Lois Armstrong, "but she's a very well-read, intelligent and genuinely optimistic person. Not that she doesn't get bitchy sometimes, but she's a bright, firm, tough lady who knows her own mind."

Barbara was particularly well-read on ancient Egypt. She could dazzle interviewers with her knowledge of King Akhenaton. "Historians think Akhenaton was the first to come up with the concept of monotheism—belief in one god, not many. It would have been so interesting to

♥ *Jeannie: 15 Years Later*, the hit NBC TV movie.

live in a society shifting their religion to something new."

Through the '70s, Barbara did make quite a few TV movies, and earned quite a bit of money doing commercials for L'Eggs pantyhose. She had a hit film in 1978, *Harper Valley P.T.A.*, and entered the '80s as a TV star again, doing a small-screen version of the film. The show was a tremendous hit—getting the best ratings of any new NBC show. But the thrill wore off quickly, and the show failed to make it out of 1981. Barbara went back to Vegas, guest-starring roles, and dinner theater productions, appearing in musicals, showing off her seldom-heard vocal talents. (Some fans may have her obscure album from the '60s, *Miss Barbara Eden*, on Dot Records.)

When the nostalgia craze became ripe, and survivors of '60s TV shows were being asked to revive them, Barbara was not amused. She didn't want to do *Jeannie* again, especially without the complete cast. When she got the new script, filled with ideas for "liberating" the genie character, Barbara balked again. She could've had a script loaded with "revenge" against Tony Nelson if she wanted, if she really believed the show had been sexist. But Barbara rejected most of the out-of-character changes.

Finally Barbara climbed back into her Jeannie costume, triumphant that she could at last show her navel. "Nobody from NBC around to look at it," Barbara pouts. "I guess they figured I'd never do anything really naughty—unfortunately."

When the movie was announced, Johnny Carson joked, "She now appears when you rub a bottle of Geritol."

He was wrong. The five-foot-four beauty was still 115 pounds, looking almost exactly as she had looked fifteen years earlier.

And how does Barbara keep herself looking like a 1965-year old? "Keeping your skin clear is the answer. I wash my face with soap and water and I rinse it right in the shower, using lots and lots of water, and rinsing, rinsing, rinsing. Then at night I use a night cream. During the day, I wash my face again and put a moisturizer on." She exercises, too. "I'm no Jane Fonda," she says, but "I like to work out doing forty-five minutes on the bicycle. But it's hard for me to make myself do it. I have to have the devil riding me before I get on."

Some old *Jeannie* regulars were back: Bill Daily and Hayden Rorke. Larry Hagman, of course, was tied up with *Dallas*. Wayne Rogers played Tony Nelson. Jeannie's fifteen-year-old son was played by MacKenzie Astin. William Asher, Liz Montgomery's ex-husband, directed. He'd directed *Bewitched*, and this one had some *Bewitched* touches. Would the young son develop genie powers (as Samantha's brood became witches)? Would the "interracial" marriage be broken up? (On *Bewitched* most witches hated mortal Darin; here an evil genie [André de Shields] plans to wreck Jeannie's marriage, complaining "Pretty soon they'll all want to marry mortals and have babies!") In yet another *Bewitched* touch, Jeannie has an evil twin sister playing childish tricks.

Jeannie was liberated, though. "Anthony, I have put my life on hold for you," she shouts.

"You used to be so pliable . . ."

"You were my master and I wished only to serve you. That is what genies are made for. But I have been doing this sort of thing since 64 B.C. and I think I am fed up!"

When Tony insists, "Have supper on the table and we'll discuss it then," Jeannie walks out into the real world.

Ultimately the message is love: "People magic is better than genie magic." And Tony finally tells her, "Loving you is the best thing that ever happened to me." But, he later adds, "The genie costume—could you wear it just for me—on special occasions." Well, doesn't Frederick's of Hollywood make money selling similar costumes to housewives?

Barbara followed *Jeannie* with national touring. "I always like to appear onstage whenever I have the chance," she says. "Even while I was doing all that TV, whenever we were on hiatus, I'd be off to tour." She played opposite John Raitt in *Pajama Game* and Robert Goulet in *South Pacific*, and did *Unsinkable Molly Brown*, *Sound of Music*, *Annie Get Your Gun*, and *The Best Little Whorehouse in Texas*.

In 1987 she made a TV movie, *The Stepford Children*, swapping comedy for horror. "Actors go through periods of doing different kinds of things," she says. "Before I did *Jeannie* everyone said, 'Can she do comedy? Is she funny?' It seems that's the way it goes."

She ended the year doing Bob Hope's Christmas special, and that was a gutsy move, not because she wore a daringly clingy gold dress in front of hundreds of sailors, but because the special was filmed in the explosive Persian Gulf. Many guests canceled out. Hope praised Barbara for staying, noting that "the words 'Persian Gulf' and the images of losing all those men scare people." In 1988 she and Hope began playing Atlantic City as a double bill.

For Barbara, the live shows go on. And for *I Dream of Jeannie*, the reruns go on and on. Barbara gets no money from it ("I sold out the rights about the third year") but she still gets fan mail from folks who love the show. Barbara knows why. It was "a very stylish piece, not characteristic of its time. It didn't fit into any groove. We weren't a mommy-and-daddy-and-two-kids sitcom or an idealized husband and wife; those were the innocent shows. Our show hasn't dated; its subject matter is sort of ageless."

Will there be yet another *Jeannie* sometime soon? Barbara smiles demurely. "Remember that bottle I lived in? It went condo."

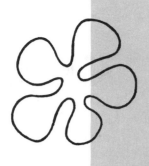

Women of Action

Anne Francis

HONEY WEST

First broadcast: September 17, 1965
Last broadcast: September 2, 1966

Her beauty mark, the mole at the right corner of her lip, was a throwback to the femmes fatales of the '30s. But as Honey West, Anne Francis could be really fatal, throwing bad guys over her back. Though she's had a tremendously long career both before and since, she's still fondly remembered for that one memorable year she played Honey West.

The five-foot-seven, 120-pound natural blonde was in show business since childhood. She was born in Ossining, New York, September 16, 1930. Never shy about her age, she upbraided writer Sidney Skolsky, "Why can't they ever get the date right?" after he'd made her a year younger, reporting the date as 1931 in a column.

Though Anne was born within the shadow of Sing Sing prison, her family heritage is true-blue all-American. Her great-great-grandfather, Tench Francis, was an aide to General Washington during the Revolutionary War, and Francis Scott Key is a distant relation.

Anne's father, Philip, was a sales manager for a company manufacturing undercoating for cars, but it was the beautiful coating on his young daughter that really made money for the family. Cover girl Anne was a model at the age of five. Artist William Reuswig drew her for the character Violet in a series of *Redbook* magazine short stories, and Mortimer Wilson modeled "Angel Face" after her in the *Sat-*

urday Evening Post. She took piano lessons at six ("I could make my living at it, if I needed to," she once said) and at seven became a child star on radio.

With prospects high, the family moved to New York City. "I was known as the 'Little Queen of the Soap Operas.' That's something for a kid to live down, isn't it?"

Little Anne was so famous she had an audience with Eleanor Roosevelt. She even had her own TV show on CBS in 1941. Of course, TV broadcasts were experimental then, and the experiment ended the following year. But 1942 was still a busy one. That year, at age twelve, she made her Broadway debut in *Lady in the Dark.* She played Gertrude Lawrence as a child. For the next three years, she starred on the radio series *When a Girl Marries.* On her fifteenth birthday, she signed with MGM for movies. Her classmates on the studio's school set included Elizabeth Taylor and Jane Powell. They got the roles; she didn't. "About the only thing I did was attend school."

She was in only one major film, Mickey Rooney's *Summer Holiday.* She had to face facts: "I was a has-been at seventeen." After all those years of evermounting success, it was tough to accept defeat. She vowed to try again in movies.

Her first marriage went "Bam." She married a movie producer named Bamlet L. Price, Jr., in 1952—the same year she made her first big film, *Lydia Bailey.* Harry Brand, the director of publicity for 20th Century—Fox, gave her a special kind of buildup. His press bio on her stressed not heat, but cool: "There is

something new in Hollywood, and 20th Century—Fox has her—a blond Mona Lisa who never allows her strikingly beautiful face to reveal her thoughts and feelings. Her name is Anne Francis and she is a tall, self-assured youngster who in repose is a perfect prototype of the classical Leonardo da Vinci portrait."

For the next three years, Anne continued making movies showing varied combinations of youthful beauty and experienced cool. Her career wasn't going too badly (*A Lion in the Streets* in 1953, *Susan Slept Here, Rocket Man,* and *Rogue Cop* in 1954). Only her marriage was going badly. Her old-fashioned hubby resented her big-bucks salary ($500 a week) and insisted she act more like a housewife than a movie star. He wouldn't let her hire a maid or cleaning woman. She divorced Bam in 1955, charging that, among other things, he "seemed to feel that all actors had a rather easy life."

She told reporters, "I discovered I couldn't be a wife and actress and do both well. Acting isn't just a part of my life, it's my whole life."

The remark was cool and analytical, but inside Anne was confused and frustrated. She sought psychiatric help to determine if acting really was her whole life. She realized it was definitely what she wanted. She stayed in therapy for five years. During that time, she went back to

♥ **The early days, billed as a "Mona Lisa" type—sweet, cool and enigmatic.**

radio and the stage, and won the part of a delinquent in the film *So Young, So Bad.* Yet, when it came time for Hollywood to film the ultimate delinquent movie, *The Blackboard Jungle,* a few years later, Anne was cast as Glenn Ford's housewife!

Studios couldn't figure out if they had a sweetheart or a siren. Anne recognized the dilemma. To a reporter in 1960 she said she didn't have "A.I.—that's a term I coined. It means audience identification." She couldn't quite make it in tough, sexy parts because "I have the wide-eyed innocence of an ingenue."

She was the only female lead in two movies, 1955's *Bad Day at Black Rock,* and the film for which she is best remembered, 1956's *Forbidden Planet.* As the ambivalent beauty Altaira, she was the darling daughter to Walter Pidgeon, but a tempting virgin to astronauts Jack Kelly and Leslie Nielsen. On *Honey West* she would own a tame ocelot. Here, she lorded over all the animals on the planet, including a fierce tiger.

The contrast between the kittenish beauty and her tiger was just one of the confusing aspects of Altaira. She was a virgin but she dressed in a miniskirt! She was bursting with curiosity—but her approach to sex was very analytical. She kissed one astronaut, then another, making comparisons. She was mysterious, distant, but obviously willing to experiment with the right man.

The innocent but sultry actress sent up conflicting signals to the gossip columnists interested in covering, and uncovering, the latest starlet. She could admit to sleeping in silken nighties, lounging in perfume-soaked bathtubs, and using sheets with lavender-scented borders. But she also mentioned that she was reading *Anna Karenina,* and was hooked on painting, writing poetry, yoga, astronomy, and eurhythmics. Her housemate was Walter Smidgeon—a poodle. As columnist Sidney Skolsky reported, "She has her fun. She is also forthright, disarmingly honest, and unpretentious."

Offscreen Anne was the very model of the emerging modern '60s woman. She was wearing slacks way before Mary Tyler Moore popularized them on *The Dick Van Dyke Show.* She wasn't afraid to talk about books and poetry, and she shunned the blond bombshell nonsense that was making Marilyn Monroe and Jayne Mansfield stars. This was still the era of the publicity stunt—but Anne was having none of it.

She got her name splashed into the papers when it was reported by press agents that she had fallen from her horse during the filming of her new movie. When reporters called her first to confirm the story, she told them it was a pack of lies.

Though a budding sex symbol, Anne was honest about her home life. The divorcée said in 1959, "Living alone as I do can be a pretty lonesome existence. But there's nothing so terrible as being lonely when you're married."

In 1960, she made her first memorable appearance on TV, starring in "The After Hours," an episode of *The Twilight Zone.* The doll-like beauty was cast as a vulnerable woman named Martha, lost and

♥ **Out of this world: Anne as Altaira, Leslie Nielsen's sensual/virginal earthy/unearthly love in _Forbidden Planet_.**

alone in a nightmarish department store after hours. There's a reason for her doll-like beauty. She is a mannequin! Her anguish is in having forgotten this, until she is brought inexorably back to the department store where other mannequins are waiting their turn to come to life and walk among the humans for a while.

Says Anne, "I still have people who walk up to me and say, 'The favorite show that I ever saw that you were in was that.' It did make a mark, it did make an impression." In his book on _The Twilight Zone_, author Marc Scott Zicree points out, "As a rule, women in 'The Twilight Zone' generally come across as drab, colorless, uninteresting . . . but Ms. Francis is an exception. There's an energy about her and a freshness, an individuality. Her performance is exciting, her reactions genuine."

Into the '60s, more filmmakers found the excitement in Anne Francis. In 1960's _The Crowded Sky_, she played a "tramp," the stewardess aboard a plane about to crash. The same year she played a call girl undergoing psychoanalysis in _Girl of the Night_. It was based on the only type of sexy best-seller available for readers at the time, the scholarly "case history," where titillating descriptions of sexual behavior were couched with detachment by professionals. Anne met with the author of _The Call Girl_, Dr. Harold Greenwald, but she was no Method actress: "Dr. Greenwald told me some places I could go to meet call girls and watch them, but if I stayed up till two in the morning looking at them, I wouldn't do so well playing one the next day after getting up at five."

The public seemed to be responding to the more dangerous side of Anne Francis. "Actresses always scramble for good roles about bad girls," she said at the time.

She married a dentist in 1960, Dr. R. D. Abeloff, but by 1963 she divorced him, charging that the doctor was "impossible to please." She won $175 a month in child support for daughter Jane, but no alimony because she made more money than he did, $22,000 in 1962.

"You would think," she remarked,

149

"that when a person makes a mistake in one marriage, the second one would work out better. But I suppose all it really proves is that a person who makes the same mistake twice doesn't have the greatest judgment in the world." Dr. Abeloff ended up trying therapy himself, but that didn't stop him from tossing a brick through his ex-wife's window one night.

Twice-divorced and thirty-five, Anne seemed like an unlikely candidate for TV stardom. As she admitted to *TV Guide*'s Richard Warren Lewis, "no really exciting things had been happening" in her career. But the secret agent fever of the era had changed a lot of rules. An obscure character actor named David McCallum was now a heartthrob playing the Russian Illya Kuryakin on *The Man from U.N.C.L.E.* An aging actress named Honor Blackman proved older was better when she turned experience to her advantage as Pussy Galore, a match for James Bond. Sean Connery, of course, was old enough to be sporting a toupee.

Anne's Honey West was the TV character closest in spirit to Pussy Galore. While Stefanie Powers was the "Girl from U.N.C.L.E." there was no "girl" in Honey West—she was all woman. Like Pussy Galore, Honey knew karate and could tangle with any man. Unlike Pussy Galore, Honey was on the side of goodness, though for this show goodness had nothing to do with the show's appeal. The show's strength was in how "bad" Honey West could be in battling evildoers.

Honey West was a semipopular book se-

ries before it arrived on TV. The character originally appeared in an episode of *Burke's Law* on April 21, 1965. She ended up cracking a case that even dapper Amos Burke was having trouble with. Audiences loved the tough, cool, sexy lady, and after that little test the show was spun into a series. For Anne, pragmatic and honest as always, the chance to do a series meant basically one thing—money. When Louella Parsons came hunting for a juicy story about the sultry star about to play a sexy detective, Anne dropped the hype: "If my personal life had worked out differently I would never have considered

♥ **Tough Stuff: Anne as cruel but kind Honey West.**

doing a series," she told the surprised gossip columnist. "But now I have to think about security for my daughter Janie and a successful series will provide that insurance."

Instead of going along with publicists and presenting the image of the sexy tigress available to all men, she was talking about having bad luck with marriage and staying at home taking care of her kid. "With experience you become aware of certain weaknesses in your character," she said. "I haven't been very smart in my judgment of husbands. I've tended to be the maternal type—to pick men I could mother. Now I have a little girl and that takes care of the maternal instinct amply. As you get older you think more carefully before you decide to spend your life with someone. At this moment I don't think I'll ever marry again."

All spies and detectives in 1965 had gadgets, and as spy shows proliferated, the gadgets had to be distinctive. CBS's new TV spy James West may have had gas bomb pellets in the heel of his shoe, but ABC's Honey West had him beat: her lace garter belt was a gas mask! And she could fire back gas bombs of her own—her earrings!

Honey West had a kind of nondescript partner, Sam Bolt, played by John Ericson, but he was less a factor to her than Artemis Gordon was to James West. For many fans, the most interesting costar on the show was Bruce Biteabit. That was Honey's pet ocelot.

Though much has been made of the imagery of "The Lady and/or the Tiger," the fact remains that very few movie sex kittens or hellcats have had a great deal of success in handling their feline counterparts. Barbara Feldon, Agent 99 on *Get Smart,* had a few years earlier achieved fame fondling a tiger—but it was a stuffed tiger. Using a real ocelot was asking for trouble. The powerful thirty-pound animal pelted Anne around with his paws, leaving her black and blue. He didn't have fangs, but he still had a strong bite. When he chomped on her hand and drew blood, she had to have a tetanus shot. Anne was less than thrilled with Bruce, though she did graciously include him in the posed photo she sent out to her fans. They seemed to want it that way.

Though she carried a pearl-handled derringer and had lethal gadgets galore, her body was her real weapon. The studio spent fifty thousand dollars on sexy outfits for her—figuring looks could kill. For the show, Anne studied Okinawa-Te two hours a day. She may have been only learning karate in real life, but on TV bad guys were flopping all over the place.

Anne was flopping all over the place, too. The show was shot at a grueling pace. Not only was she expected to put in the usual eighteen-hour days at the studio, she had to perform a lot of the fighting stunts without a double. Her arms and legs were littered with bruises, her muscles were sore. Finally, so was she. She began to fight with the studio big shots who were blithely ordering her into battle. One day on the set she balked at the orders and shouted, "Don't rile me, because I'm ready to swing!" They backed off.

As she explained at the time to *TV Guide*, "I am now able to release a healthy temper when necessary. Before analysis, I was basically a passive person. When I was a kid, I was very much afraid of anger of any sort. I was brought up so young to please everybody; to show anything but a smile was considered sinful. Coming out of analysis . . . I realized I could make things around me change."

On Friday nights, viewers tuned in for James West and CBS's *The Wild Wild West* at 7:30 and stayed tuned for *Hogan's Heroes* and *Gomer Pyle*. ABC's *Addams Family* had run out of gas and was buried by *Hogan's Heroes*. The Addams clan was not a good lead-in for *Honey West*, and ABC decided to drop the show, rather than shift it to a better time slot.

Anne was nominated for an Emmy that year. There were only two others nominated in the Best Actress in a Dramatic Series category, Barbara Parkins of *Peyton Place*, and the winner, Barbara Stanwyck for *Big Valley*.

Anne resumed her movie career, making *Brainstorm* and *The Satan Bug* in 1965, and had a juicy role in *Funny Girl* in 1968—until prima donna Barbra Streisand cut it down to size. With Anne's face all over the cutting room floor, The *Newark Evening News* reported Anne's part as "the smallest costarring role ever filmed . . . a total of four lines."

She made *Impasse* in 1969, along with *The Love God* and *More Dead Than Alive*, but her career didn't ignite. She attempted directing in 1970, beginning with a modest movie short, hoping to pro-

duce wholesome films. She had adopted a second child and explained, "With two small children at home, I'm very concerned about the quality of shows a child can watch." Anne pointed out that for a "sex symbol," she had always been pretty wholesome, never really embarrassing herself in a sleazy cheesecake part. Her appeal was the fascinating difference between her hot looks and her sometimes coldly diffident manner.

In 1972 Anne adopted another baby. She still wasn't married, and her two other children were still young—Jane was nine and Margaret, a year and a half. She said, "I believe there's a psychological time for women to have children. I don't believe it would have been better to wait until I get married again—if I ever do get married again."

For a while, Anne Francis, so capable of appearing strangely aloof in haunting roles in *Forbidden Planet* and *The Twilight Zone*, was content to be haunted by her own house. In 1973 she told the *National Enquirer* that there were some ghostly goings-on at her Brentwood home. "There was a lot of frightening banging and clattering," she said. "It sounded like someone was trying to rip the room apart with an ax."

She told the *Enquirer* reporter that she believed in the spiritual world, and that "everyone has psychic ability but many do not realize it." It seemed that the apparition had centered itself on her three-year-old daughter Margaret. It was her room where all the banging and clattering occurred. And earlier, some kind of creature evidently had been paying close attention to the child: "I came home from work one afternoon . . . there in the middle of the patio was a perfect circle of little red clay footprints. But there were no footprints entering or leaving the circle, and there's no red clay in that area. I guess they were made by an invisible playmate of Maggie's."

Ten years later, after lecturing to college audiences and at holistic centers, Anne wrote *Voices from Home: An Inner Journey*. It was largely about her experiences with the supernatural, which included a prenatal vision of her father, the time as a child that she "mirrored" a mean neighbor's gaze and caused the person to suffer a mild heart attack, and, of course, her experiences with creatures in her house.

In 1986 Anne staged a minicomeback, appearing as Farrah Fawcett's aunt in the miniseries *Poor Little Rich Girl*, and as a swimsuit-clad drunk in *Laguna Heat*, an HBO suspense movie.

"The cycles are fascinating in this business," says Anne. "It's a roller-coaster ride." She talked about some of the other scripts she's been given recently. One had "a lot of vulgarity for vulgarity's sake. They keep on saying that it's the end of an era. And I don't mind it, if only the new era would start. It's time for some more films with substance. Filmmakers are hung up on the innards of cars instead of the innards of movies."

Despite the problems with Hollywood

♥ **The '80s are hot for Anne, starring in HBO's *Laguna Heat*.**

movies, and the occasional problems with haunted houses, Anne professes to be at peace. "Quite honestly," she says, "I wouldn't be brokenhearted if I didn't marry again. Having a man doesn't work unless the strength and will to survive are there within yourself first. The mistake people make about love is trying to find it in others without finding it in themselves first. . . . It comes down to the individual responsibility within our own individual worlds. That's how to achieve heaven on earth. We come onto this planet alone and we leave alone so it becomes our responsibility to spiritually grow to the best of our ability. And the first step is to understand forgiveness within ourselves."

Stefanie Powers

THE GIRL FROM U.N.C.L.E.

First broadcast: September 13, 1966
Last broadcast: August 29, 1967

After nearly a dozen minor movie roles, Stefanie Powers had a dream: fame and fortune in TV. She was hoping "to be just right in a part, so people will say, 'Remember Stefanie Powers in . . . ?' "

For over a decade, she got her wish. "Remember Stefanie Powers in *The Girl from U.N.C.L.E.?*" people asked. Now there's a generation gap among Stefanie Powers fans. Quite a few young ones say "Remember Stefanie Powers in *Hart to Hart?*"

Stefanie Powers was a powerful star on TV in the '60s, and she's a powerful star now.

Like powerful stars of old, Stefanie had to change her name to become famous. Born in Hollywood on November 2, 1942, she was Stefania Zofja Federkievicz. To her parents, she was simply Stefka.

After they divorced, Stefanie lived with her mother, who had no objections to the girl's interest in the movies: "My family knew some of the people in the film industry and I had often been on sets as a kid. At the time I was growing up, there was something of a campaign going on to find replacements for Shirley Temple and Margaret O'Brien. It was fairly common for young girls to be brought to studios for interviews. Nothing came of mine, though, and by the time I was in junior high, I was thinking more about becoming an Olympic swimmer. I gave that up when

I developed so many muscles that I began to look like a man."

She looked quite womanly by the time she got to Hollywood High. Calling herself "Taffy Paul," she joined the cheerleading squad. But Stefka was no model cheerleader. One night she and four guys snuck out to play practical jokes. "We cut down a tree and painted a bench green . . . very subtly, four police cars pulled up . . . we were arrested for . . . I think they call it mischievous mischief."

The girl was thrown out of school, but later reinstated. After graduation she began auditioning for movies. She nearly won a part dancing in the film version of *West Side Story,* but, following a few obscure films, she was officially introduced to filmgoers in *Experiment in Terror* in 1962. She played a slightly plain, slightly baby-fatted high schooler—kidnapped, forced to strip to her slip, and then locked away for the rest of the movie. The story was about big sister Lee Remick's attempt to rescue her. Mostly, Stefanie got to stare and snivel.

She got a big break when a TV series about the film business, *Hollywood and the Stars,* did an episode about the life of an average starlet and chose her to follow around. After 1962's *If a Man Answers,* she got to play John Wayne's daughter in 1963's *McLintock!* and Tallulah Bankhead's victim in 1965's *Die! Die! My Darling!*

In true starlet fashion, she was interviewed about her sleep habits. Gossip columnist Sidney Skolsky confided to his readers that she didn't sleep nude, but wore "thin feminine nightgowns. She has no trouble getting off to sleep." She was quizzed about her pet cat named Kat, and her dating. Early on she firmly deflected questions about her personal life ("Eddie Fisher is a very nice person and a dear friend but I'm not ready yet for any kind of a serious romance . . .") and stressed that she was not interested in pretty bimbo parts in movies: "I want to act. I love to act . . . I just hope there will be things I can do in the future that I will believe in."

She couldn't believe in *Love Has Many Faces* or the sorry remake of *Stagecoach* she did. She recalls now, "My career was going nowhere. It was becoming stagnant. It wasn't that I was making B movies— they were multimillion-dollar productions. They just weren't any good. I kept making trips to London and I began to think of going to work for the National Theatre." The trouble was that the theater paid next to nothing.

Instead, she tried TV.

The producers of the tongue-in-cheek spy series *The Man from U.N.C.L.E.* were looking to spin off a sequel—something hip for the late '60s. Instead of a Brylcreemed Robert Vaughn they had tousled Noel Harrison as Mark Slate. And instead of cute David McCallum, they wanted a cute female spy—a Honey West, only trendier and maybe British: Stefanie Powers as April Dancer. Stefanie had lived in England, and sounded just British enough to American ears.

"Even my friends tell me I'm putting on

♥ A budding starlet: Dean Jones has good reason to stare at Stefanie in *The New Interns*.

airs because of my broad *a*. Believe me, I'm not. It came about because I learned English as a second language. I spoke Polish before English."

Stefanie's slight accent and British-model look were important. Otherwise the producers would've gone with their first choice, ex–Miss America Mary Ann Mobley. "It did not work well with her," Stefanie reported, "so they changed the concept."

If the producers were looking for a woman who really had the strength and skill to make bad guys say uncle, they would have chosen Stefanie anyway. Part of the five-foot-five-and-a-half 120-pounder's regimen was morning calisthenics straight from the Royal Canadian Air Force booklet. She often got up at 7 A.M. for a three-hour run. She was a fine water-skier and an able swimmer. She enjoyed race-car driving and didn't need the prop department to supply her with a cool car—she owned a Marcus 1800 that Steve McQueen envied.

She had credits well suited to the outlandish plots of *U.N.C.L.E.* shows. Strange but true, Stefanie co-owned a Mexican bull breeding company, and once actually faced a snorting bull in the ring. For practice, she sparred with cows. "I've never fought an animal and killed it," she explained to writer Richard Warren Lewis, "but I've killed in a slaughterhouse . . . you take a sword and with one swift stroke sever the spinal cord. It's instantaneous death."

On *The Girl from U.N.C.L.E.*, the accent was on lighthearted adventure and dastardly villains. Taking a step backward from *Honey West*, the Girl from *U.N.C.L.E.* would be a girl—getting into trouble and generally needing a man to bail her out. "It's Red Riding Hood," producer Norman Felton told reporters. "The girl is real, the wolf isn't." He wanted April Dancer to be feminine: "A girl who's looking for someone to hit doesn't appeal to me." *TV Guide* noted, "The ladylike April is not required to kill the bad guys. Her feminine charms serve as the bait . . . her partner provides the fireworks."

Look magazine agreed she was "a kind of Little Orphan Annie in Bondage" who "shys away from rough stuff." And Stefanie herself added, "I'm the bait to catch the agents of Thrush. I lure them to our traps . . . [then] I can run to the ladies' room."

If April Dancer couldn't even talk her way out of trouble, Stefanie could. Unlike her often helpless heroine, Powers could speak seven languages: Polish, English, Spanish, French, Italian, German, and Russian. She's since added some Arabic, Portuguese, Mandarin and Swahili.

Leo G. Carroll, who played *U.N.C.L.E.*'s chief Alexander Waverly, performed double duty on the old and the new shows. The others were not so sure. David McCallum, "this year's teen fave" during *U.N.C.L.E.*'s heyday, didn't want to make guest appearances on the show. "Look at it this way," he told reporter Tom Mackin, "the new show might take off, and we might go downhill . . . I certainly don't want to be a party to my own destruction."

The show was scheduled for 7:30 P.M.—the idea was to go for the teenage girls who had temporarily made David McCallum a *16* magazine "fave," and the boys who bought millions of bucks' worth of *U.N.C.L.E.* bubble gum cards, lunch boxes, and toys. April and Mark would be on the kids' fantasy level; more Nancy Drew and one of the Hardy Boys than John Steed and Emma Peel (*The Avengers* was popular in England at the time, but had yet to appear stateside). The most important thing about April Dancer was the costuming—the show spent a thousand dollars per episode on the proper Carnaby Street miniskirts and femme fatale gear. That's all it was: "gear." As in "fab."

The Girl from U.N.C.L.E. gave young '60s girls the very rare opportunity of watching a female fantasy figure in action. April Dancer was naïve, like they were, got into danger (her TV tortures

♥ **When fans, like the author, wrote in for a shot of Stefanie in *The Girl from U.N.C.L.E.*, this is what came in the mail.**

could easily be a fantasy extension of a tough homework assignment), and got to wear the great outfits Mom and Dad wouldn't let her buy even for her Barbie doll. Young girls could also imagine sexy but pal-like Noel Harrison coming to their rescue. Boys who had enjoyed the camaraderie between Napoleon Solo and Illya Kuryakin now realized how much more fun it could be if their partner in danger was a girl!

Like its predecessor, *The Girl from U.N.C.L.E.* was an offbeat mix of camp

and drama. Today, both shows have trouble holding up. Much of the humor seems lame and the drama kid-show obvious. One of the most memorable shows had Boris Karloff playing "Mother Muffin," owner of a waxworks. Says Stefanie, "I think you could safely call Boris Karloff in drag campy."

Very few shows have been able to appeal to both hip and square audiences. *Batman* only did it for a few seasons. *The Avengers* also had a short run. *U.N.C.L.E.* had been fading and spy shows like *Secret Agent* and *Amos Burke, Secret Agent* were already dead. *The Girl from U.N.C.L.E.* lasted just one season. *The Man from U.N.C.L.E.* was disarmed a year later.

Despite *The Girl from U.N.C.L.E.*'s short run, fans have a long memory for it. The *Girl from U.N.C.L.E.* paperbacks and novelty items that desperately flooded the marketplace that year are now highly prized. Today there are *Girl from U.N.C.L.E.* fanzines that chronicle every episode of the old show.

At the time, the death of the TV show nearly meant the death of Stefanie Powers's career. "When *Girl from U.N.C.L.E.* bombed, I didn't work in this town for two years. . . . It was a baptism of fire. . . . I was sort of shell-shocked by it. I didn't think I could ever speak another line of dialogue with an ounce of humanity, and I felt personally destroyed. So I left the country."

Stefanie was married to Gary Lockwood (the former Gary Yurosek, a fellow Pole). He was making movies in Europe, and

♥ **Silly doings in spyland: the Girl from U.N.C.L.E. says "Uncle!"**

that seemed like the ideal place for an extended honeymoon. "I think it'll last," Stefanie told Nora Ephron (then a reporter for the *New York Post)*. "That's stupid to say, I know. Anyway, we're bound and determined to stay together even if it doesn't work. We're never getting a divorce."

Gary and Stefanie were divorced in 1974.

Gradually Stefanie began turning up in guest roles on TV shows. Once her career was back in shape, and people were no longer talking about how memorable she was as the "Girl from U.N.C.L.E.," she decided to plan her next move. "I've had

every disease known to man on every medical series that was ever done," she told *TV Guide* in 1977. "I'm through having diseases. The acting profession for women obeys a law of diminishing returns. I have only a few more years to make it. Do I want to end up in my forties worried about whether or not I'll get a week's work on some cop show? Do I want to fall heir to all the emotional tragedies of a mature woman who becomes aware of the diminishing attraction of her physicality? Does it mean I better start thinking about a few lifts? A little surgery?"

Did it mean having to do a new TV series called *The Feather and Father Gang?*

It was a comedy-detective series. She played "Feather," a lawyer. Harold Gould was "Father," an old con artist. The idea was that legally and semilegally, they could always defeat the baddies. The mild show drew mild interest and folded in six months. Stefanie scored better in a six-part miniseries, *Washington: Behind Closed Doors*, which included Robert Vaughn among the star-studded cast.

The next time Stefanie did a comedy-detective series, she wasn't playing opposite her "father." She was opposite Robert Wagner in *Hart to Hart*. They attracted. This time she had a hit.

Hart to Hart, premiering in 1979, would become one of the most popular shows of the '80s, lasting half the decade (a phenomenal run in the new TV era of limited attention spans and intense turnover).

"I never thought of anyone to play my wife other than Stefanie Powers," Robert Wagner recalls. "We worked previously in an episode of *It Takes a Thief* and I liked her a lot. Her style of acting is perfect for me."

Many considered the show a modernization of the *Thin Man* movies, since Robert and Stefanie, as the jetsetting Jonathan and Jennifer Hart, took a sophisticated, witty attitude to their crime solving. Like Nick and Nora Charles, they displayed as much personal charm as detective ability, and a lot more romance than was permitted back in the '30s and '40s.

Some thought the romance was real between Wagner and Powers, but Robert was married to Natalie Wood and Stefanie had gone from Gary Lockwood to William Holden. She met Holden while separated from Lockwood in 1973. Together they traveled the world. With her language fluency and adventurous nature, Stefanie had always been a globetrotter, owning an apartment in Hong Kong as her special "get away from it all" retreat. With Holden, she discovered Africa, sharing his love and respect for the land, the animals, and the people.

They visited Lake Turkana, "inhospitable as hell, a barren place, but I never felt more serene in my life." They publicized the artwork of the Papua natives of New Guinea, airlifted supplies to the starving children of Kenya, and created a wildlife preserve. At home, Stefanie brought her wildlife with her—she shared the house with a cat, two dogs, a parrot, and a monkey.

The combination of Holden and Powers seemed an odd one, given their twenty-four-year age difference, but aside from age, they were very much alike, both unique and iconoclastic. "We didn't gravitate toward each other because we were eager to jump into bed, although we did that too, but because we sensed the possibility to have an important exchange between two people. Bill lived a life of privilege [but never] lost his enthusiasm, his curiosity, or his innocence."

Tom Mankiewicz, a director on *Hart to Hart*, remembers what happened on November 16, 1981: "We'd just finished shooting out at Malibu when word came over the radio that Bill Holden had been found dead. Stef'd just left for home, and we were concerned she'd hear the news on the car radio, which she did. We all went over to her house that afternoon. She was remarkably strong through her loss . . . she was magnificent. Remarkably strong."

Less than two weeks later, Natalie Wood was dead. The Wood and Holden tragedies were blockbuster news. Both deaths were untimely and tragic. The press reports on the drinking habits of both stars made for lurid speculation, and the pressure on Stefanie—as lover to Holden and costar to Wagner—made her the target of an unbelievably intense media blitz. Wagner also had to bear up under the twin strain of private grief and the public's "right to know." Stefanie remembers, "When double tragedy struck we were bonded together, Robert and I were a great help to each other. It would have been very hard to get through otherwise."

When she was able to leave her duties on *Hart to Hart* she flew to Kenya, where she stayed, alone, for two months.

In 1985 the network lost heart with *Hart to Hart*. Robert Wagner remembers, "She cried for a day."

She says, "I miss the family feeling we had for nearly six years. It was a shock. There was no warning. We just weren't on the schedule anymore." She adds, "We're all big kids, and this is a big business. What am I supposed to do—jump out a window? It's not cancer research."

Stefanie became a TV movie and TV miniseries star, playing Maggy Lunel in *Mistral's Daughter*. She accepted the challenge of aging both backward and forward (from eighteen to sixty), and handling the steamy and/or ludicrous love scenes. In the show, Stacy Keach played a character who loved painting her nude and licking her toes ("You know, you have very beautiful feet"). Timothy Dalton's character liked trailing a flower all over her body before the big seduction. Gossips speculated on a romance between the ex–"Girl from U.N.C.L.E." and the choice for the new James Bond, speculation fueled by the stars' refusal to dignify the leering questions.

After *Hollywood Wives, TV Guide* reported that Stefanie "bloomed like a rose in a slag heap," as the one "actress who best rose above her material" during the year's TV movies. She went on to star in *Deceptions*, taking on the difficult dual role of twin sisters Stephanie and Sabrina. Bored housewife Stephanie swaps identi-

ties with jet-setting Sabrina after insisting "I need to get away from New Jersey." Amid the lurid doings, affairs, deaths, and deceptions, both lifestyles chalk up pluses and minuses. "I have met twins who have given me corroborative evidence that something like this could be true," says Stefanie. "And in fact some more intimate stories from one woman who actually was dating one twin and having an experience with the other and couldn't tell the difference . . . it's a fascinating idea . . . something I think probably all of us would have some fantasy about doing, given the opportunity."

From slightly ridiculous soap operas with elements of challenge in them, Stefanie was thoroughly challenged by the 1987 miniseries *At Mother's Request*. She played Mrs. Frances Schreuder, who was convicted of masterminding her father's murder—which was committed by her son.

Stefanie used "the Method" to make the part work: "The whole notion was that I was not trying to find myself in the character but to lose myself in her. I had to adopt her speech pattern, her walk and her mannerisms so that I could be relieved of any image the audience had of me as a known figure." Coworkers remember how deeply she went into that character. Even after the director yelled "Cut!" she remained either murderously cool or as tensely coiled as a rattlesnake.

Coincidentally, Stefanie's friend Lee Remick was also starring in a multipart version of the sordid tale. But when Richard Behrens (a figure in the real-life

♥ **If looks could kill #1: a deadly role in *At Mother's Request*.**

murder case) visited both sets, he came away believing that Stefanie's portrayal was closest to the real Mrs. Schreuder. He found her "perfect for the part," marveling at how she picked up even minor character details, like the way Schreuder smoked her cigarettes.

When the show aired, the *New York Post* reported "Powers' iceberg mother makes Joan Crawford in 'Mommie Dearest' look like Shirley Temple." *The New York Times* later added that her portrayal was so "frightening, monstrous and so relentlessly villainous" it dwarfed the frail script and even made the sensational murder uninteresting by comparison.

These days, gossip columnists are more interested in how Stefanie's love life compares to what it was with William Holden. "Why is everybody so terribly concerned about my boyfriends? Sure I have them, but I haven't met anyone who's a reason either to change my life or to adjust to his. I don't feel that a companion will give me something I lack;

I think that in a true relationship one has to be deeply in love. It has to be an amalgamation of spirits, an agreement to be together out of choice, not out of need. It doesn't make sense to me to be with someone just for the sake of having a man in my life. I have a lot of friends, and I don't feel lonely at all, so, unless I fall desperately in love, there's no reason to change what I do."

Stefanie has been able to do as she pleases professionally. She can get dramatic roles, but that doesn't mean she isn't still capable of playing a beauty in light soap opera roles. As she proved with her recent book *Superlife!* she's as attractive as ever, and determined to stay that way.

Some figured she was just jumping into Jane Fonda's leotards hoping for lookalike sales figures. She admits, "My first reaction [to doing such a book] was, 'It's just what the market needs, another actress writing a fitness book.'" Then she realized how unique some of her methods were. She told readers about her "grape fast" diet. Eat nothing but grapes for a week—"Select one variety of grape, one color only . . . one pound of grapes for

each of three meals daily." After the week, gradually add other fruits, then vegetables, then low-fat cottage cheese.

She explained both physical and mental well-being. She advocated twenty-five minutes of exercise a day (mostly yoga-style stretching and balancing) and even insisted on a healthful approach to showering: "Let hot water run down your front and back in this standing position: Head back, shoulders and chest dropped, pelvis tilted forward and up, knees slightly bent." She had advice on avoiding stress, borrowed from Dale Carnegie: "When a situation makes you anxious, ask yourself: 'What's the worst that can happen?' This helps put matters into perspective."

Stefanie is now a complete actress, still capable of playing a "Girl from U.N.C.L.E.," but also adept at playing an aunt, mother, grandmother, mistress, or any other female. As the "Girl from U.N.C.L.E.," Stefanie trotted the globe pursuing fantasy adventure. Today, she travels the world more often than any spy, playing polo for charity in England, making films in Europe, supervising William Holden's work at the African animal sanctuary. She doesn't need '60s fantasy adventure—now she has the real thing.

Diana Rigg

THE AVENGERS

First American broadcast:
March 28, 1966
Last American broadcast:
September 15, 1969

She was the very first famous actress to do a nude scene onstage. She was one of the first to openly oppose marriage and bear a child out of wedlock. She made the move from '60s TV sex symbol to one of the '80s most respected actresses.

Americans' fascination with Diana Rigg began with *The Avengers*. As Mrs. Emma Knight Peel she had a cool, wryly appealing British accent and an indulgent, worldly smile. Slim and sexy, she was paradoxically both S *and* M, the karate dominatrix in black leather *and* the heroine in bondage. All this before most people knew what S&M meant!

All this before people learned that the very name "Emma Peel" was a pun on British slang: "M (male) appeal."

Fans gasped at Diana's beguiling beauty, but she always had a down-to-earth view of herself: "The shoulders are extremely wide and very square, and the breasts don't compensate for this width. The hips are too wide. The arms and wrists are slender, but the knees and the calves are over-developed. The jaw is much, much too strong and the mouth is too small."

As a child, she and her family moved from Doncaster, England (where she was born July 20, 1938), to Jodhpur, India. Her father, a civil engineer, warned her to avoid the miserable streets around her, and never play with stray dogs. They were probably rabid.

♥ **Submissive . . . and dominant!
The two sides to Emma Peel in**
The Avengers.

At eight she was sent back to York-
shire, only to be stifled in strict boarding
schools. At the Fulneck Girl's School in
Pudsey, "We were never allowed to talk to
boys. It was so strict that you even had to
wear your hair according to orders. It had
to be a precise length. Then they used to
inspect our gym slips which had to be exactly two inches above the knee when we
were kneeling down."

As a teen, she rebelled against the discipline, and was constantly in trouble
with school authorities: "I was tall and

redheaded. Tall redheads always got
caught."

She appeared in school plays, inspired
by her father, who had often read stories
aloud to her. When Mr. Rigg at last returned from India, Diana happily ran up
to him, saying she loved him more than
anyone else in the world.

He answered, "You must never feel
that about anyone. It's an unrealistic way
of living."

She eventually chose an unrealistic
way of living. Her father thought she'd

settle down and marry. Instead she attended the Royal Academy of Dramatic Art and developed "a guiltless approach to relationships outside marriage."

Diana waitressed and modeled to help support herself. In 1959 she joined the Royal Shakespeare Company, but often her attitude was less than classical. In *Macbeth* an actor was required to slip his hand just inside her bodice. Diana made the most of this, unnerving him by whispering, "Up a bit . . . left a bit, down a bit . . . golden shot!"

Later, playing Cordelia to Paul Scofield's King Lear, Diana found tragedy to be high comedy. To get through the long show, Scofield drank a healthful brew of malt, bran, wheat, and honey. "He suffered from flatulence as a result," Diana recalls with a prim smile. Odd sounds accompanied his impassioned cries of "Howl, howl, howl! O, you are men of stones." The audience wept, the actors sniffed the air in confusion, and Diana, a great actress, lay dead in his arms when she really felt like doubling over with laughter.

After five years of the classics, Diana felt restless. "The trouble with staying with a classical company is that you get known as a 'lady actress.' No one ever thinks of you except for parts in long skirts and blank verse."

After she did a TV production called *The Hot House,* Diana and dozens of others auditioned to replace Honor Blackman in *The Avengers.* Blackman was leaving her role as tough karate queen Cathy Gale to play Pussy Galore in *Gold-*

finger. Diana remembers, "We were told to turn up in black trousers and sweaters. We looked like a neofascist army . . . I had not seen *The Avengers* when I was cast but the idea of doing a television series that was a little wacky and way out appealed as the perfect antidote."

Adding cleverness and class to the karate, Emma Peel became John Steed's choicest companion, earning seven hundred dollars a week, a mighty sum for an actress on British TV. The deal didn't include royalties.

When the show was imported to America, spy-weary critics applauded the show's tongue-in-cheek attitude. The staid *New York Times* even approved Diana's switch from "Lear to Leer."

Diana was one of the very few liberated women in movies or TV. Most, like Honor Blackman's Pussy Galore, were karate-chopping hellcats *only* until melted down by a conquering male. Diana was independent without being strident. She could even be John Steed's superior without wrecking his ego. In one episode he joins Ransack, an intellectual organization she belongs to—but he's only able to join because she took the IQ test for him!

Diana Rigg was like Emma Peel. "No man will ever conquer me or make me his slave," she said at the time. "Nobody owns me, nobody will. I don't yearn for security. Marriage might be fine for many people, but I find its permanence appalling."

The British press was astounded that she was living with Philip Saville, a married man. Even if his estranged wife ac-

♥ A towel-clad cutie in *The Assasination Beauty.*

cepted divorce, Diana wouldn't accept marriage. "Living together" before the term was even popular was typical of Diana's freethinking.

The jumpsuits Diana wore on the show, with white stripes down the side, were marketed as "Emma Peelers." When she came to the States, a reporter called her a trendsetter in women's fashions. "Yes, I know," she said. "But you Americans still don't admit women to your restaurants in a trouser suit."

Rigg's liberated attitude never turned off her fans. They sensed she wasn't fighting for liberation, she'd won it. Some were a problem, though, taking away her

equality by putting her on a worshipful pedestal—for her beauty, for her intellect, for Emma Peel's strengths and/or weaknesses. "I must say it was great fun at first being recognized on the street . . . but I'm really not equipped to be a celebrity. I loathe intrusions on my privacy . . . and the autograph syndrome is simply beyond my comprehension." Once she stopped an autograph hound by admonishing, "It's illegal to sign autographs in the street."

Letters poured in from awkward lads twisted into knots over the worldly wise spy, letters that seemed to say, "Mrs. Peel . . . you're needed." Sometimes they'd get an answer—from Diana's mother! "My daughter is much too old for you," she'd write, "and what you need is a good run around the block."

Some episodes required more than that. Especially with Emma's exotic outfits and the dialogue's innuendo. Steed visiting the head of a cat owner's club:

"The name of your beloved pussy?"

"Emma."

"Coloring?"

"Reddish brown."

"Oh! A cuddly tabby . . . what a joy it must be when she's curled up in your lap."

Often Emma had to deflect the sweaty innuendo herself. Interrogating a tattooist who asked if she wanted a rosebud tattoo ("one on each"), she neither wisecracked nor lectured, just continued her interrogation. When a shoemaker moaned "I am at your feet!" and begged her to wear "kinky black leather," she kept her professional dignity, allowing only a mild gaze of tolerant disdain.

Perhaps the best analysis of Emma Peel was given by berserk film director Z. Z. Von Schnerck (Kenneth J. Warren) in an episode written by Brian Clemens: "I needed you, Mrs. Peel, a woman of beauty, of action, a woman who could become desperate and yet remain strong, a woman who could become confused and yet remain intelligent, who could fight back and yet remain feminine. You, and only you, Emma Peel, have all these qualifications."

The Avengers played with the two extremes of the Emma Peel character. Fans fondly remember when she played a harem girl wearing a flimsy costume of frothy veils. The most annoying thing about it for Diana was that, in deference to censors, she had to wear a glass jewel to cover her navel. And it kept popping out. The episode gave dramatic proof that Diana was far from busty—but that her enthralling attitude and personality made up for the lack of standard showgirl charms.

Yes, she wore slave trappings in one episode—but in another, around the same time, she wore the opposite. At the "Hellfire Club," she wore a heartstopping dominatrix outfit, a one-piece black leather corset, a choker collar of nails, garish eye makeup, and thigh-high leather boots. A whip completed the ensemble. Somehow Emma and Steed's cheeky chic and understated chemistry and professionalism helped keep the show on the right side of "good clean fun."

Diana was nominated for Emmys twice. Both years she lost to Barbara Bain of *Mission: Impossible.*

Seeking new challenges, Diana gracefully exited the series in an episode that introduced her substitute, Linda Thorson. A traditional baby-faced doe-eyed brunette, Linda's Tara King was often a bumbling burden on Steed. Comparisons with Emma weren't complimentary and the show soon folded.

Diana pursued films recklessly, starring in classics and schlock, creating "a checkered record, to put it baldly." Her best remembered films were *A Midsummer Night's Dream* and *On Her Majesty's Secret Service.* The latter starred George Lazenby as James Bond. He was no Patrick Macnee. The two stars had a passionate loathing for each other. Lazenby called the filming "hell," noting Diana deliberately ate garlic before the love scenes. Diana loathed her costar's inflated ego and crude demands for preferential treatment.

In retrospect, the whole thing was a mistake. Whether it was Lazenby, Connery, or Moore, James Bond was a hokey smirker with *Playboy* party-joke wit. Though she played Bond's love, not a bimbo, Diana still could do little with such a classless character. Summing it up, she said, "Bond is the symbol of the man who finds women expendable. He throws them away . . . I don't think you'd want to spend more than five minutes with him. He's an egomaniac."

Diana dazzled the theater world in June 1970 with a role that called for elegance,

♥ **'60s free spirit.**

sensuality, humor . . . and nudity. For this retelling of *Abelard and Heloise*, reporters flocked to get a glimpse at the undress rehearsals. Diana was surprised and disgusted to have her "art" treated as a striptease show. While she protested, the British press jeered at the pretensions and leered at the protrusions.

Diana and actor Keith Michell were under tremendous pressure. "All the press

in London were down on us, most of them without having seen the play. *Hair* had already been in London with its nude scene but no one knew those kids and no one minded them undressed." But this was Diana Rigg. This was Emma, unpeeled.

"I see no point in being defensive about eroticism," she said firmly. "I think it's rather good to have it. But if people care to see me as a sex symbol then they'll have enormous problems confronted with *me.*"

Diana only antagonized the press with such outbursts. She tried humor. She tried to downplay the nudity by pointing out that her body was no different from *any* other slim young woman's. "I have to make up my backside," she confessed. "Otherwise when I show it onstage it looks like a piece of old cod."

On Dick Cavett's show, she recalled the incident and added, "My body is no different from anybody else's. In fact . . . I remember one letter particularly that said, 'I don't know why you bother. My girlfriend's tits are much larger than yours.' You see? But everybody who steps onstage has to have the definitive figure. But in the play a definitive figure is neither here nor there, you're playing a character."

The love scene was done in semi-darkness and was only a few minutes long. As Diana told Cavett, the hardest part was hitting the stage: "You're fully dressed until the wings. Then you drop your knickers. That's easy. Stepping onstage without your knickers is the most difficult thing in the world . . . I promise you, it is, if you've ever done it, it's against everything you've ever been taught. And the draft is incredible . . ."

But at the time, she was dismayed that "the press was there from all nations . . . panting as if I had another breast and he had two penises." It was only after the reviews came in that she was vindicated. *The Times of London* bowed to her beauty ("she looks handsome, she always does

when that auburn mane tumbles over her shoulders") and then to her bold acting ability ("it was a gritty, aggressive performance, daring the house to laugh at lines which from the mouth of a less assured actress would have provoked schoolboyish titters").

The play premiered in America in March of 1971—to a replay of the abuse and controversy from England. Critic John Simon wondered if the nudity was called for, since "Diana Rigg is built like a brick mausoleum with insufficient flying buttresses." The more serious critics disagreed. Clive Barnes in *The New York Times* called the controversial three minutes "the most tasteful, tactful and apposite nude love scene I have ever encountered. As a matter of record I suppose Miss Rigg and Mr. Michell are the first major stars to appear naked on the Broadway stage, but . . . the scene is neither prurient nor distasteful." Barnes added that Diana was "perfect, as sensuous as a cat, with hidden fires beneath the surface." Diana won a Tony nomination for her role. In 1972 she made pulses jump in another play, *Jumpers*, with another nude scene. When Diana joined Sir Laurence Olivier's National Theater Company, he affectionately nicknamed her "Tits" Rigg, not for the nude roles, but for her habit of not wearing a bra.

The next time Americans saw her, it was in her underwear. *TV Guide* ran a photo of her with her dress down, exposed in her red slip. The caption read, "Avenger tries on a TV role . . . not to mention a skimpy dress."

She was starring in *Diana*, a new TV show. "After two years at the National Theater I was heavily in debt to my bank." Besides, the '70s was a new time and she was going to break new ground. She said her TV character was "probably the first divorcée on television . . . she's very sophisticated, in her thirties, with lots of boyfriends. And she's not untouched by human hands."

Diana was as refreshingly uninhibited as ever. At a *Los Angeles* magazine cover shoot she suddenly struck a pose, quipping "How does that grab you? A crotch shot! How about a bum shot?" And, with good-natured pique, she called out, "How does *Los Angeles* magazine feel about nipples? I'm not wearing a bra and this sweater's a bit thin. NBC doesn't like nipples at all, or navels, or any manifestation of humanity."

As Diana Smythe, fashion coordinator for a big department store, she had a zany cast of coworkers and funny friends visiting her apartment. It seemed like a poor copy of *The Mary Tyler Moore Show*. Diana's enthusiasm soon waned, driven down by bad scripts and tedious filming schedules: "It's an outrage to sit in a makeup chair at eight A.M. and have someone make up your face. It's almost obscene. You've just got up. You're at your most tender and vulnerable. My face doesn't take kindly to makeup at eight A.M.!"

The bold, liberated character Diana expected to play was "revised" before filming began, and saddled with wimpy boyfriends and other bozos. "After filming the second episode," she sighed, "I knew it was going to be garbage." It was canned in five months. "I had never known such failure on such a grand scale . . . if you embrace failure it's rather less painful. That's one of the best lessons I've ever learned."

Diana refused to replay glamour roles in spy films. "I couldn't live the life of some plastic movie queen or sex symbol," she said at the time. "Whatever happens I won't fall into that trap. I've always done the most ridiculous, extreme things. Whatever I do, it's because my appetite is right for it . . . I like to get some enjoyment out of what I'm doing.

"I need antidotes to relieve boredom," Diana added. "It appeals to me to be erratic. I think it's unfortunate that they— the critics, the audience and sometimes other actors—insist that you be consistent."

In 1973 she met an Israeli artist, Menachem Gueffen, at a party. That's Menachem, with "the rich gargling ch as in Hanukah," as *TV Guide* reported. A member of the Israeli army Palmach, he knew more moves than Emma Peel ever did. Their turbulent relationship was marked by many skirmishes. Diana recalls one major battle: "We were in a hotel six floors up. I told him I was leaving. He said, 'Fine, I'll help you pack.' He did. Then he picked up my suitcase and all my clothes and threw them out the window. I was amazed."

After that, she said, "I seriously felt I'd met my match." Menachem recalls the incident as a turning point, too. After he dumped the suitcase out the window, "She became very calm, very quiet . . . and very obedient." They married. The calm and obedience ended. "We quarreled all the time. To her not quarreling was not relating."

The divorce, in 1974, was wrenching. She came to Broadway for *The Misanthrope.* "To go on living for me is to go on learning," she said. "Learning about life and everything that makes life. Wanting to go on learning makes one vulnerable of course. You are always exposing yourself to risk. I hope I can take it."

She played bitchy, sexy Celimene in the play, and told her costume designer Celimene should "be wearing golden browns and creams, never any underwear. Her body has to be evident, fluid, nothing stiff to imprison her personality."

Offstage Diana explained her love theories to writer Lawrence B. Eisenberg: "I refuse to say 'I love you' in order to legitimize the fact that I've been to bed with a fellow. I don't expect him to say it to me, either." Admitting to many different lovers '60s-style, but adding '70s maturity, Diana remarked, "Sex is wild improvisation and shouldn't be taken too earnestly at the beginning. It is, after all, only one way of communicating—a very enjoyable one at its best—but then you get to a much deeper communication, which is not necessarily commitment, but just the trust of being together continuously." She didn't dwell on the problems of sex, insisting, "The sex act is the funniest thing on the face of this earth . . ."

It was fun to visit a transvestite bar near the theater and talk with the queens. A gay club proclaimed her "the woman we would most want to turn straight for."

But it wasn't funny when her name was linked to men as diverse as middle-aged Alec McCowen, a young black actor named Clifton Davis, and fifty-one-year-old businessman Marvin Liebman, among others. It wasn't funny when interviewers treated her badly: "If you are an actress you're expected to be . . . stupid, vain. Well, we are intelligent. The nature of our work demands it. I'm not exactly all teeth and tits, am I?"

When Diana took *The Misanthrope* to Washington, D.C., she was invited to a White House dinner. After doing a matinee and an evening performance, she was tired out. During the formal dancing, she slipped and fell. Others were aghast, but not Diana. As she describes it, "Well, my dear, I saw the top of President Ford's head and the back of Mrs. Ford's head and that was too fucking sobering so I took to the dance floor and landed flat on my ass."

Diana was down but not out. Not when she was having such a good time not acting her age. She posed for a London tabloid with her skirt flying upward à la Marilyn Monroe, and said, "Ever since I was a young girl, I knew I would reach my peak at around age thirty-five. Well, I'm thirty-six, and unlike so many other women, glad to admit my age . . ." She vowed to grow into "a sexy, crazy old lady."

She had a new love, ex–Scots Guard Archie Stirling. They didn't marry, but that didn't stop Diana from giving birth to daughter Rachel Atlanta at the age of thirty-eight. Again, she was a trailblazer in "scandal," but ignored the tabloid headlines. "I had worked solidly for eighteen years," she recalls, "and by that time I had become aware that the career just wasn't going to be enough. Pregnancy, and all that came with it, was enjoyable, relaxing. The comparative quiet in one's life that follows having a baby."

In 1979 Diana returned to the stage in *Night and Day*. Of 1981's British TV version of *Hedda Gabler*, the *Daily Mail* declared, "There is nothing remotely brick mausoleum-ish about her, and buttresses are well hidden by Victorian crinolines." Diana could look back at the old "brick mausoleum" criticism and laugh: she put it in her book *No Turn Unstoned*, an ironic collection of actors' bad notices.

In 1982 the gracefully maturing actress came to America for *Colette*, a surefire musical by the team that wrote *The Fantastiks*. It opened in Seattle—but fell apart before reaching Broadway. Once Diana came apart, thanks to her costar, a deaf white cat. It bit her.

"I bled profusely, but my main concern was the negligee I was wearing . . . I had to hold the hand and the damned cat as far away as I could so as not to drip blood all over it and ruin the thing."

The show died in Denver, but Diana made a big splash when she got to New York, anyway. She and Archie Stirling asked Manhattan city clerk David Dinkins to marry them in a quick ceremony. Once again, Diana's lighthearted attitude astonished the British press. When she arrived in London, she said calmly, "We got married to liven up a dull Thursday."

Diana's career hasn't been dull lately. She did *Heartbreak House* on stage in 1983, *Bleak House* for *Masterpiece Theater* in 1985, and *Follies* in London in 1986. She concluded 1987 acting in the TV movie *A Hazard of Hearts*, based on a Barbara Cartland soap opera.

She enjoys soap operas and *Follies*, even if critics only want her in Shakespeare. "Deep down I have an irreverent spirit. . . . People who take themselves deeply seriously are really good at tragedy, and I don't take myself that seriously. . . . I could have gone on and done greater and greater things . . . but I didn't. It's as simple as that."

As for *The Avengers*, Diana's view is tolerant. She rarely watches the show. The last time she did, she found the young Diana Rigg far removed from the current version. It was "OK." Of course, the show's rabid cult thinks it's still more than OK—many fans are still enthralled by the very modern antics of Emma Peel. "When I get touchy," she says, "it's at the suggestion that *The Avengers* was the sum of my professional career."

Now fifty, she says, "I'm not sure that I like the thought of decline. I've got to come to terms with that, with bodily decline. I'm not at all sure in what way to go forward into the next part of my life."

Diana would like to see more new plays with important roles for women: "The real difficulty is finding vehicles for the ladies. There aren't very many new parts for us. I don't know why.

"I think we're fascinating creatures."

♥ Diana, the very image of class,
and still elegant in the '80s.

Index